MAY 2 2

TO WEAVE—
THE SWEDISH WAY

TO WEAVE—
THE SWEDISH WAY

New Techniques and Modern Projects

Arianna Funk
Miriam Parkman

PHOTOGRAPHY: Campher – Larsson & Ankarfyr

TRAFALGAR SQUARE
North Pomfret, Vermont

First published in the United States of America
in 2021 by
Trafalgar Square Books
North Pomfret, Vermont 05053

Originally published in Swedish as *Att väva*.

The instructions and material lists in this book were carefully reviewed by the author and editor; however, accuracy cannot be guaranteed. The author and publisher cannot be held liable for errors.

ISBN: 978-1-64601-085-1
Library of Congress Control Number: 2021945454

Photography: Campher—Larsson & Ankarfyr
Interior Graphic Design: Gustav Skoogh & Mikael Hultman
Swedish Editor: Elisabeth Fock
Translation into English: Arianna Funk

Printed in China
10 9 8 7 6 5 4 3 2 1

Foreword

For a long time we each harbored our own secret dream of writing a weaving book, and when we finally confided in each other, it seemed obvious that we should write one together. We attended the same weaving school, sat next to each other for years in the same studio, and weave with the same kind of loom. But what—and more importantly, how—we weave as professional weavers is completely different. There is more than one way to weave, perfection isn't required, and there aren't any rules about which techniques you should use. However, there are some ways of going about the weaving process that are commonly accepted, because they are logical and ensure a good result. In your own weaving practice, you'll learn from many teachers and role models, and you can adopt the way one of them threads their heddles and the way another beams on in order to create fantastic works from your own brain.

We gather much of our inspiration from older weaving books and traditional techniques, but we are forward-thinking when it comes to color, potential uses, and design. In this book, you'll find a foundation upon which to build your own way of weaving. We offer complete projects that you can follow to the letter, but also chapters on textile design and how to find and refine your own aesthetic.

ARIANNA: Weaving has been a part of my life ever since my mother asked my father to build her a quilting frame ... and received a Swedish-style floor loom hand-built by my father and grandfather instead. This was in the late 1980s in the US, and I have many warm childhood memories of visiting fiber festivals and Weaver's Guild meetings. As an adult, I first chose an academic career in fashion history and wanted to work with museum collections. But when I moved to Stockholm, I decided to go back to school yet again in order to create my own context in my new country. After weighing many options, I realized that three of the women I admire most were avid weavers, and I decided to apply to the Friends of Handicraft School. My first semester there, everything fell into place: weaving is what I am meant to do.

I mostly weave what are called *bruksföremål* in Swedish, a term I like to translate as "working textiles," and flossa, a knotted pile technique, is my favorite way to weave. I'm most energized by the weaving process itself—it's the techniques, drafting, problem solving, and throwing the shuttle that are the core of my interest. The craft, defined as mastery of technique and material, is what I value and focus on in my process.

MIRIAM: Textiles have held deep and important meaning for me as long as I can remember. Among my earliest memories is the agonizing feeling of wearing something in a color or shape that I didn't like. Both of my parents work for the Swedish Church, and when I was growing up, I often hung out in the vestry after the service and watched while my dad hung his stole and chasuble among all the other church textiles. I remember the colors and gold embroidery as clearly as the smell of cold stone and candle wax, of coffee hour with juice and homemade baked goods among the sturdy pine furniture and hand-woven, hand-embroidered curtains and tablecloths. The minute the thrift store Erikshjälpen opened we would be there, and my mom bought piles of old handwoven bedclothes for 50 cents or a dollar each. I began to buy clothing at thrift stores in middle school, and I've collected clothing and objects from the 1930s to the 1960s ever since. When I found out about the Friends of Handicraft School a few years after I graduated high school, the penny dropped—weaving was the way I could express everything that was in my head.

I see the warp as a clean piece of paper to fill, using the magical equation where by itself a thread is only a thread, but many threads together become a unit. A woven piece can be decorative and philosophical at the same time, equal parts ancient and futuristic. That's powerful!

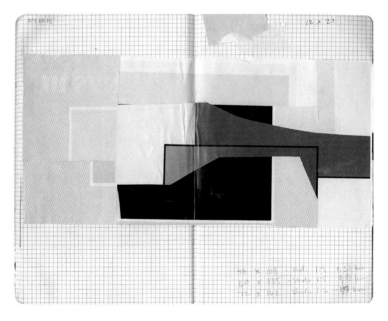

I often make sketches in collage for my rugs. This is the sketch for my very first flossa rug, seen in the picture on page 6.

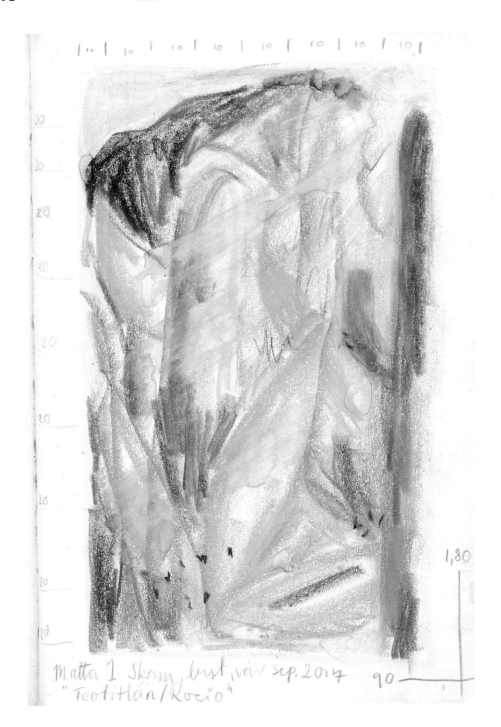

Sketch made with water-soluble pastels that depicts cacti, agave, corn-
fields, and sun-drenched valleys in Oaxaca, Mexico. Intended as a sketch for
the tapestry on page 6—read why that didn't pan out in the design chapter!
—Miriam

To Start

There are as many ways of weaving as there are weavers, and you'll eventually find a combination of different ways of going about it that best suits your personality. You may have different starting points for your weaving projects: you can begin with an idea for an item you want to create, a certain material, or a certain technique. Test out our methods, read older weaving books, and ask your weaver friends how they do things.

If you've never woven before, a beginner's project with step-by-step instructions can be found starting on page 12. The instructions there can also be used as a reference guide for future projects. Weaving is a process with many steps—you don't have to remember all of them from day one. It's also important to remember that weaving is so much more than just sitting and throwing a shuttle back and forth or tying knots. Good planning is the name of the game in order to achieve the results you're aiming for, even if you're going to weave freely in the simplest warp.

TECHNIQUES

There are three primary techniques in weaving: plain weave, twill, and satin. Plain weave is the simplest, more compact and firm than the other two. In plain weave, the warp and weft threads cross often and in a consistent, orderly fashion. Plain weave only needs two harnesses and 2 treadles on a floor loom. Twill has slightly longer floats, a clear diagonal directionality, and requires at least 3 harnesses and 3 treadles. Satin is the supplest of the three, has even longer floats, and is therefore best if you want to work with smooth surfaces. Satin requires at least 5 harnesses and 5 treadles. Almost all other weaving techniques are variations on these three.

WOOL, COTTON, AND LINEN

You can weave with a wide range of different materials, but in this book we use three basic natural materials: wool, cotton, and linen.

WOOL is a wondrous material that warms in the winter and cools in the summer. It basically washes itself and only needs to be aired out as long as the material isn't completely soiled. What's more, wool is water-repellant and rarely stains. Wool is also elastic and very forgiving to weave with; it's easy to achieve good tension in the warp. If the yarn is plied and spun with long fibers, wool yarn is very strong. Sweden produces a lot of wool yarn, and there are many different gauges available. We think it's important to support local yarn producers and therefore we used yarn made of Scandinvian wool as much as possible for the projects in this book.

COTTON isn't the most eco-friendly material, but it's easy to find organic cotton in Sweden (even if it's not produced within the country). Cotton is elastic, absorbs water well, and is relatively inexpensive. Great for towels and similar items you'll use often. Keep in mind that cotton shrinks quite a bit the first time it's washed.

LINEN has a beautiful shine and absorbs liquids well. It becomes stronger when it's wet. Linen is a sustainable material: good for the environment, long-lasting, and hard-wearing (as long as it's not creased too firmly).

TOOLS

- **LOOM**
  (we use countermarch floor looms in this book)

- **BENCH TO SIT ON**

- **REEDS**
  Start with 8-, 10-, and 12-dent

- **SHUTTLES**
  Both boat shuttles and rug shuttles

- **BOBBIN WINDER**
  You'll also need bobbins or paper to wind yarn onto

- **WARPING MILL**
  Or warping board

- **THREADING/SLEYING HOOK**

- **LEASING STICKS, BEAM STICKS, & TEMPLES**
  These should be able to cover 12 to 36 in / 30.5 to 91.5 cm

- **BALL WINDER & SWIFT**

- **SEWING MACHINE & HANDSEWING TOOLS**
  Sewing needles, thread, pins for finishing

- **SCALE**
  For weighing yarns

- **SCISSORS**
  Larger scissors for cutting fabric and thicker material, and thread snips for cutting rya pile

MORE ADVANCED TOOLS:

- **FLOSSA RULER & FLOSSA KNIFE**

- **FOR DYEING**
  Pots (that you use exclusively for dyeing), thermometer, dyestuff, chemicals, large spoons/sticks, drying rack, precision scale

Weave Tea Towels, Step-by-Step

The first project we will weave is a tea towel in a warp-faced twill, with cotton in both warp and weft. The description that follows is a set of general instructions for how to set up a weaving project, with details specific to this project used as examples.

To make the towel the right thickness and to make it absorbent and hard-wearing, I've chosen Ekelunds organic cotton 8/2 in two different colors. That way you can test both checks and stripes and see how the warp and weft colors meet in the weave structure. There will be 5 stripes of orange (#225) and 4 stripes of ecru (#1218) in the warp. A useful standard size for towels is 19½ × 27½ in / 50 × 70 cm.

Cotton shrinks and draws in quite a bit, so each towel should measure 21¼ × 29½ in / 54 × 75 cm in the loom to compensate.

We wrote this book in Swedish, using the metric system. That means some of the numbers, when converted to the imperial system, might be a bit intimidating, with lots of fractions. We've listed the original numbers alongside so that the patterns are more accessible.

Our advice for those of you who exclusively use the imperial system is to follow certain parts of the patterns without worrying too much about the details. For example, use the number of ends we give, round the sett to the closest whole number, and don't worry if your project ends up being slightly bigger or smaller than our example. Or maybe a weaving length includes a fraction—round that up, since you always need a little wiggle room in a warp anyway. Trust your instincts, make it easy for yourself, and always make a sample if you're unsure! It's a good habit to adopt if you haven't already.

CALCULATE THE WARP

I've woven with this yarn many times before and know that a reasonable sett for this project is 24 epi / 10 epcm. That means that for a towel that is 22½ in / 54 cm wide in the loom, we will need 540 ends.

Number of ends = sett x width in the reed

For a rough estimation of sett for a yarn that you haven't woven with before, you can use this method: Wrap the yarn around a ruler so that it covers a whole inch (or cm), with the wraps close to each other but not crowding. Count the number of wraps. For a tabby weave, use a sett with about half as many ends as there are wraps per inch / cm. For example, if your yarn has 30 wraps per inch, you should have a sett of 15 epi (equivalent to approximately 12 wraps per cm = 6 epcm). If you're planning on weaving twill, which is a bit looser than tabby, use a sett with ⅔ as many ends as wraps (20 epi / 8 epcm, in our example). For satin or other looser structures, use a sett with ¾ as many ends as wraps (22¾ epi, rounded up to 23 / 9 epcm, in our example). Round up or down to the closest whole number—I promise it won't make a noticeable difference. I like my weaving to be on the tight side, so I usually add 2-3 ends per inch (one end per cm). Always make a sample, if you've had to estimate the sett!

To calculate the warp length, we begin by calculating the length of the weaving you want to make. Here, I'm using the tea towel measurements.

FABRIC (3 TOWELS, 29½ IN / 75 CM LONG INCLUDING HEM)	59 IN / 225 CM
SAMPLE	7¾ IN / 20 CM
TOTAL WEAVING LENGTH	66¾ IN / 245 CM

Then we can use that information to calculate the warp length:

WEAVING LENGTH (FROM TABLE ABOVE)	66¾ IN / 245 CM
5% TAKE-UP	4¾ IN / 12 CM
LOOM WASTE	39¼ IN / 100 CM
TOTAL WARP LENGTH	110¾ IN / 357 CM

We've calculated the warp length as 110¾ in / 357 cm, which we can round to 110 in / 360 cm. These measurements can also be written as 3 yd / 3.6 m.

If you'd like to add fringe or other finishing details that require extra warp length—for example, a braided edge for a rug—don't forget to add that as a row in the warp length table above.

Now that we know that the warp is 3.6 m long, we can calculate how much yarn we will need, which we will measure in kilograms. If the warp is striped, like in our tea towel project, you calculate each color separately. Refer to the warp order on page 34 to see how many total ends of each color we need. We will use metric measurements here.

Number of ends x warp length in meters = total meters of yarn you need

```
300 ENDS ORANGE X 3.6 M = 1080 M ORANGE
240 ENDS ECRU X 3.6 M = 864 M ECRU
```

We can use the number of meters to figure out how many kilograms of each yarn we need:

$$\frac{\text{NUMBER OF METERS NEEDED FOR THE WARP}}{\text{THE YARN'S METERAGE/KG}} = \text{NUMBER OF KG NEEDED FOR THE WARP}$$

The 8/2 yarn we use in this project is 6400 m/kg.

$$\frac{1080 \text{ M ORANGE}}{6400 \text{ M/KG}} = 0.168 \text{ KG, OR } 168 \text{ G ORANGE NEEDED FOR WARP}$$

$$\frac{864 \text{ M ECRU}}{6400 \text{ M/KG}} = 0.135 \text{ KG, OR } 135 \text{ G ECRU NEEDED FOR WARP}$$

CALCULATE WEFT

Calculating the amount of weft you will need is good planning, for either staying on budget by buying only as much yarn as you need or making sure your stash yarn will last the whole project. If you haven't woven a project before and don't know how many weft picks per inch or cm you'll have, in many cases you can anticipate the same number of weft picks per inch or cm as you have warp ends per inch or cm. Thus, in our tea towel project, we can estimate 24 weft picks per inch / 10 weft picks per cm. Here, for simplicity, we will also only use metric measurements.

Number of picks per cm x fabric width in meters x weaving length in cm = meters of weft yarn you need for the project

```
10 WEFTS/CM X 0.54 M FABRIC WIDTH X 256 CM WEAVING LENGTH =
1382 METERS WEFT NEEDED
```

To calculate the number of kilograms of yarn needed, you can use the same formula that you used for the warp above.

$$\frac{1382 \text{ M WEFT}}{6400 \text{ M/KG}} = 0.216 \text{ KILOGRAMS, OR } 216 \text{ G OF WEFT YARN}$$

When I wove these towels, I actually ended up with 20¼ weft picks per inch / 8 weft picks per cm, which required 0.172 kilo (172 g) of yarn. I bought 200 g to be on the safe side. As with the warp, if you're planning on weaving with different colors in the weft, you calculate each color separately.

LET'S WARP!

When you warp, you establish the length of the warp and the order of the colors or different threads you're using.

Warp with two ends in your hand. If you only have one cone or ball of the color you're going to use, make another ball that weighs about half of what you need to warp with so that you have two sources to draw from. Do the same with each of the colors you need for the warp.

The following description is for a warping mill, but you can also use a frame. Begin by making a "measuring thread" in a color that contrasts with the warp, the same length as the warp (110 in / 3.6 m, in our case) plus a little bit extra for tying with. Begin by tying the measuring thread to the top peg. Spin the mill with one hand and let the measuring thread run along the mill relatively horizontally until you get to the final peg, where you build what is called the cross (see the top photo on page 18). You may have to adjust the pegs on your mill to get the correct length, and if needed, add a few inches or cm, but don't ever warp less than the calculated length. I never warp more than about 12 in / 30 cm of warp width at a time, which helps ensure good tension while beaming on. The warp for our tea towels is 22½ in / 54 cm wide, so I split it down the middle and planned to warp two chains, each with 270 ends.

Most important while warping is to hold even, moderate tension the whole time. Preferably you'll warp all the chains for a warp the same day.

Now it's time to make the actual warp. Tie your ends of the same color together (in our case, we start with orange), lay it over the top peg, and follow your measuring thread.

Just as you did with the measuring thread, spin the mill with one hand and hold the threads you're warping with in the other. If you hold your pointer finger between the threads, it reduces the risk of tangling (see the top photo on page 18). When you come to the three pegs at the other end of the measuring thread, you'll make your cross. The cross is the most important part of the warp, and it keeps all the threads in order throughout the entire preparation and weaving process. When you get to those three pegs, the warp should run: over one peg, under two and reverse, over two and under one. Then the warp follows the measuring thread up to the first peg again, where it runs under that peg and turns to go back down again (see the top photo on page 18). Repeat until you have the correct number of ends of each color. You can always secure the "active" ends and count how many

Warping on a warping mill. My spool rack is behind me, on the same side
as the hand I use for warping.

The cross, where the warp ends cross each other during the warping process.

A very hard tie-off in the middle of the warp.

ends you've warped so far. The easiest way to do this is at the cross. You can also tie a counting thread loosely around 100 ends at a time at the cross so that you don't have to re-count all the threads each time.

If you need to make a join in the yarn, it's best to do it at either the first or the last peg, or at most 4 in / 10 cm from the peg, so the joining knot doesn't end up in your woven fabric.

When you're on the last pass of the warp, split the two threads and tie them around the peg. You can do this on either the first or last peg, depending on how many ends your warp has.

Now: the very important step of tying off. We tie off the warp so that all the ends stay in place and don't tangle during the following steps of the weaving process. I prefer to use pre-cut lengths of very strong yarn (such as linen warp yarn), between 4 and 8 in / 10 and 20 cm. Tie four knots around the cross so that it doesn't disappear when you remove the warp chain from the mill; these don't need to be tied tightly. Then thread one tie through the warp that loops around the peg at the other end, so that everything stays in order while beaming on. Then tie a number of regularly spaced, very tight knots along the warp, which will help keep even tension while beaming on (see the bottom photo on page 18). I suggest about 29½ in / 75 cm between each knot along the length of the warp, and preferably exactly the same spots on each warp chain, but the actual interval between knots isn't so important.

At this point you'll either need to be very limber or recruit an assistant, because when you remove the warp from the mill and make a big chain, it's good to have a little resistance. Hold the warp tightly with one hand at the first peg (the opposite end from the cross), and remove the peg so that the loop is free. Thread your other hand through the loop, grab the whole warp, and pull the loop over your hand (see the photo on page 20). Continue until you come to the cross, where you'll tie the last loop down. Do NOT pull the cross into the chain, let it hang free; both because you don't want to make a knot with the warp but also because we're going to use the cross in the next step. Lift the whole chain off and lay it on a table with the cross easily accessible.

PRE-SLEYING

When you've warped all the chains you need, lay them next to each other in the correct order on a table.

For this step you'll need: the correct reed, a sleying hook, a reed

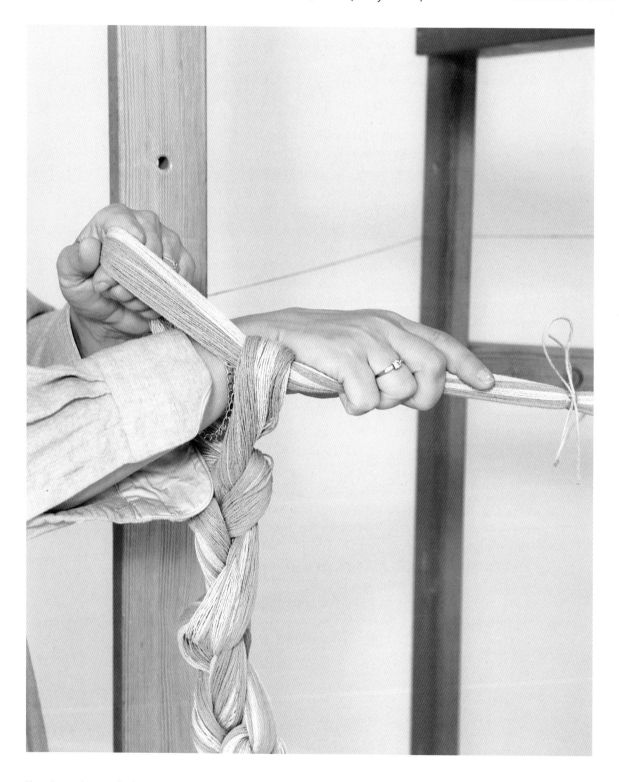

How to make a chain with the warp.

holder, weights (can be heavy books), two pairs of leasing sticks, and a tape measure. Thread one pair of leasing sticks through the holes that were created when you tied off each side of the cross. Tie the leasing sticks together at both ends so that the cross is secure, and after that you can remove the strings you tied the cross off with. Put the reed in the reed holder between you and the cross, and the other pair of leasing sticks between you and the reed (see the photo below).

Pre-sleying spreads the warp ends evenly over the width of your project. In most cases, you can use the same reed that you'll use later when weaving. But if the reed you're going to be weaving with is tighter than 50/10 or 12-dent, it's best to use a reed that is twice as sparse for pre-sleying (if you have one).

For these towels, we need a 12-dent / 50/10 reed. That number means that there are 12 dents per inch / 50 dents per 10 cm (5 dents per centimeter). When we sley the reed later, in the loom, we want to end up with 24 epi (10 epcm), and with a 12-dent / 50/10 reed, that means we will sley 2 ends in each dent. But when you pre-sley, you're working with the loop that was created at the end of the cross, i.e. four warp ends that can't be separated. Use the sleying hook to pull a loop through the reed, and create a new cross on the other side by

Pre-sleying in action. The cross is re-created on the second pair of leasing sticks (in the foreground) after drawing the ends through the reed.

The warp is placed in the loom. When spreading the warp over the back stick,
you may have to take the cords on the back stick into consideration.

twisting the loop and placing it on the leasing sticks in front of the reed. It doesn't matter which way you twist them, but you must be consistent. Since we have four inseparable warp ends, leave an empty dent in between each loop. When you've pre-sleyed the whole warp, tie the new leasing sticks together so the new cross is secure, and you can remove the first pair of leasing sticks. Now you're ready to put the warp in the loom.

PREPARING TO BEAM ON

In preparing to beam on, you'll arrange the warp in the loom so that it's centered, even, and easy to beam on. It's easiest with an assistant, but you can do it without one. One tip is to tie loops of strong, inflexible yarn around the top crossbeam near the back of your loom so that the leasing sticks have a place to hang out while you're working. Put the reed in the beater with the leasing sticks toward the back of the loom and let the warp chain(s) hang over the breast beam for now. Some weavers like to roll or jack up the harnesses so that they're not in the way, but I just push all the heddles to each side and make room so the warp can be beamed on freely. Stand at the back of the loom, carefully pull the leasing sticks toward the back beam, and hang them in those loops you hung up earlier. You may have to release one of the tie-offs in the warp in front of the reed to allow the leasing sticks to reach all the way to your back beam. Thread the back stick (from the yarn beam) through the loop at the end of the cross and spread the warp evenly over the project's width (see the photo on page 22). This step is easier if you have an assistant who can hold the warp chains, if you hang weights from the chains, or if you wind the chains around the breast beam so that you've got a bit of resistance when you are spreading out the warp. Make sure that the back stick is sitting evenly in its cords, that the cords are running straight up from the yarn beam to the stick, that the warp is the right width according to the draft, that the warp ends are equally spread out on the stick and run straight back from the reed, and, finally, that the warp is centered.

Make sure your loom is locked in a neutral position while you're working. If you have a countermarch, make sure the pin that locks the top lamms is in place, and put your shafts in holders or lock them if preferred. Collect some beam sticks or thick paper that is wider than your project and fetch at least one person who can help you beam on!

1. SHAFTS/HARNESSES
   WITH HEDDLES

2. LAMMS (BOTH SHORT
   & LONG)

3. BACK BEAM

4. YARN BEAM
   The warp is yarn
   on this beam

5. TREADLES

6. FABRIC BEAM
   The warp will have
   become fabric on
   this beam

7. BREAST BEAM

8. KNEE BEAM

9. REED

10. BEATER

11. TOP LAMMS

Beaming onto my Öxabäck countermarch loom from A.K. Snick-
eri. The warp was long enough
that it could begin under the
front crossbeam. Miriam has her
foot on the beam to be able to
keep tension with her entire
body weight.

BEAMING ON

Of utmost importance when beaming on is that your assistant keeps consistent, even tension. They don't have to hold so tightly that their knuckles turn white, but the harder they pull, the easier it will be for you to discover any tension issues. With a warp like the one in our tea towel project, one person can hold both warp chains. If the warp is wider, it's better to have multiple assistants for more even tension. While they are holding the warp chains, they should remove the ties as you go along, and try to be as consistent as possible with the tension the whole time. They shouldn't let the warp glide through their fingers, but rather move forward along with the warp and adjust their grip as needed. If the warp is long enough, you can begin by letting the warp run over the breast beam and under the crossbeam at your feet—the more points of contact, the better the tension (see the photo on pages 24-25). Your assistant(s) should say stop when they need to adjust their grip, move further back on the warp, or rest their hands. You should run your hand over the warp at the back of the loom every now and then to check that the tension is even across the whole width, and always after your assistant(s) adjust their grip. Try to beam on as much as possible with the same grip. Move the leasing sticks forward every now and then so that they don't go over the back beam.

At the beginning, your assistant(s) should only hold light tension while you wind the back stick and warp down to the yarn boom. The tension becomes most important when the warp has gone a whole rotation around the yarn beam and the warp begins to layer onto itself. Put a layer of sticks or paper between the yarn beam and the first layer of warp so that the warp ends lie as flat as possible on the beam. The next two layers can be beamed on without sticks or paper, and then if you have more warp to beam on after that, you can place a stick approximately every 15 cm or 6 inches to re-create that flat foundation for the warp ends and ensure even tension.

Toward the end of the beaming-on, it gets a little more difficult to hold even tension, so try to draw on the last 12 inches / 30 cm in one go, until the end of the warp has just passed the breast beam. Your assistant(s) should keep holding the warp until you've hung the leasing sticks in their resting loops again, and if you have a short warp that didn't even get all the way around the yarn beam when you beamed on, use masking tape or string to secure any beaming sticks so they don't slide down when the tension is released. Now your assistant(s) can gently let go of the warp. Don't forget to remove the tape or string around the sticks after you've tied the warp on later in the process.

THREADING

Threading establishes the order of the warp ends, and which shafts will raise or lower which ends.

Cut the loop at the end of the warp, pull the ends out of the reed, and make a loose slipknot with sections of the warp. If I have two warp chains, as in this project, I make a slipknot with each of them; that way, I know where the center of the warp is. Remove the beater, the breast beam, and maybe even the knee beam to make room. Both you and your leasing sticks should be as close to the heddles as possible when threading. You can make two more loops with scrap yarn, shorter this time, and hang them from the castle so the leasing sticks can hang right behind the heddles. Sit comfortably, preferably on a lower bench or chair, so that the heddles are slightly below eye level. Threading is a demanding task, in terms of time, concentration, and the toll it takes on your body, so pause often to stretch.

Keep this book open next to you or photocopy the draft on page 35 and tape it to the loom, so you can look at the chart while you're threading. The threading chart can be found at the bottom of the draft, under the drawdown. In this pattern, it's called "straight draw," which is the most common threading pattern. In Swedish drafts, Shaft 1 is the furthest up and Shaft 4 is at the bottom. Shaft 1 is furthest from you, and Shaft 4 is closest to you, both on paper and while sitting at the loom (but not while IN the loom).

Begin on the right side, with the heddles grouped and waiting at your left hand; pull them back to center if you parted them when you beamed on. Then pull out one heddle from each shaft to work with. You can even place them slightly diagonally to imitate the black squares in the threading draft (see page 35). Pick up the first four warp ends with your left hand—the cross fulfills its destiny here and shows the order in which you should pick them up and thread them—and pull one thread through each heddle in order, 1-2-3-4. Repeat until you've threaded all the heddles. It's helpful to make a loose slipknot with bundles of 8 threaded ends as you go along.

The draft on page 35 doesn't show all of the stripes in the warp, since the threading is repeated over the whole width; we can instead write "x4" under the section that will be repeated. That means the indicated section should be threaded a total of 4 times, plus the last stripe = 9 stripes total.

SLEYING

When it's in the beater, the reed is what beats the weft into the warp, but it also spaces the warp ends out evenly across the project width. We've chosen a 12-dent / 50/10 reed, and if you want 24 epi / 10 epcm, you should pull 2 ends through each dent. I hang a loop on each side of the upper shaft bar closest to me and place the reed there, so it hangs freely right below the heddle eyes and warp ends. Measure the middle of the reed, then measure out half the width of your project (in our case, 11¼ in / 27 cm) to the right of that center point. Begin to thread there, so the warp ends up approximately in the middle of the reed. Tie bunches of 20 sleyed ends (10 dents) together in a loose slip knot under the reed. 20 ends equals about ¾ in / 2 cm of width in the reed, which is a good measure for tying on with later.

If you have added extra ends as selvedge reinforcement, they should be sleyed together with the outermost "normal" warp ends. We aren't using extra selvedge ends in our tea towel project.

Put back all the beams and crossbeams that you removed in order to thread and sley comfortably, and put the reed in the beater. Check that the warp is centered in the beater by measuring from the selvedge of the warp out to the edge of the beater (not the edge of the reed) on both sides. Adjust until the warp is equidistant from both edges of the beater.

Threading with a threading hook. The ends that have been threaded are to the right of my hand, and those waiting to be threaded are to the left.

TYING ON

Tying on is the process of tying the warp ends to the front stick, thus tensioning the warp in preparation for weaving. It's important to be meticulous and picky here, since even tension is the key to success-ful weaving. You'll tie on in two rounds, one preparatory and one final. Pull the front stick straight up from the fabric beam, over the knee beam, and under and around the breast beam until it meets the knot-ted bunches in the reed. Find the center bunch (or pair of bunches) and divide it (or each of them) in two. The right-hand section goes over the stick, and the left-hand section under the stick. Tie them in an overhand knot (see the top photo on page 31). The end that is pointing up is wrapped once more around the tensioned warp ends and pulled downward (see the bottom photo on page 31) to lock the overhand knot in place. Do the same with the bunch furthest to the right, the bunch furthest to the left, then the bunch that is immediately to the right of the center bunch(es) and the bunch immediately left of the center, and so on. Don't worry if the tied-on bunches end up a little unevenly ten-sioned in this preparatory step.

In the final tie-on, you tighten up and fasten these bunches, and the order is slightly different this time. Begin in the middle again and remove the "lock" so that you only have the overhand knot again. Tighten the overhand knot as much as you can, and repeat the lock. This time it's secured even more by pulling the other end (not used the first time) over the first lock and pulling it downward. Repeat with the bunches directly to the right of the center, then directly to the left, and continue like that out to the selvedges. The center bunches will tend to end up slightly looser, which you can prevent by tightening the fabric beam cog wheel one or two teeth after you've tied 4-6 in / 10-15 cm across the width in each direction.

LEVELING THE WARP

Level out the warp with a thick linen warp thread (preferably 8/5) or doubled cotton rug warp 12/6. Tie the thread to the hole on the left side of the front stick, and then thread it under all the ends that run under the front stick and over all the ends that run over the front stick. Pull the thread as taut as possible and tie it to the hole on the other end of the stick. Beat once or twice with the beater.

The tie-on method begins with an overhand knot.

The next step in the preparatory stage of tying on. The end that is pointing upward in the overhand knot is wrapped and pulled down to temporarily "lock" the knot.

TIE-UP

The tie-up determines which shafts will be raised and lowered when you step on each treadle. In Swedish drafts, you'll find the tie-up at the bottom right corner of the draft (see page 35 for the tea towel draft). You read the tie-up from right to left, with Treadle 1 furthest to the right.

The tie-up shows which shafts should be tied up to which treadles. Just as with the threading chart, Shaft 1 is at the top and Shaft 4 is at the bottom. Each treadle has a series of holes or a metal rod that is used for tying the treadle to the lamms between the shafts and the treadles. A filled/black square in a Swedish tie-up chart means that the shaft is lowered. In a counterbalance loom, this is achieved via a cord tied directly from the treadle to the lamm. The empty/white squares are ignored. Countermarch looms have two lamms for each shaft, one short and one long. Where there are filled/black squares, the treadle should be tied to the short lamm (which lowers that shaft) and where there are empty/white squares, the treadle should be tied to the long lamm (which raises that shaft). Remember that when you're sitting IN the loom to tie up, you should be reading the tie-up draft upside down.

WEAVING

We can finally weave! First, however:

■ Check that all the warp ends are at the bottom of the heddle eye when the loom is in a neutral, locked position. When you pull the pin out of the top lamms on a countermarch loom, the shafts will sink slightly, and the ends should end up approximately in the middle of the eye.

■ Check that all the shafts are hanging freely and not in holders or locks.

■ Step on a treadle to create a shed, pull the beater gently toward you, and check whether the warp touches the beater at the top or bottom edges of the reed. If so, raise or lower the beater so that the warp runs freely.

Wind at least one bobbin of the yarn that you're going to use, as well as a smaller bobbin of scrap yarn that's slightly thicker than the yarn you'll be weaving with. If you're weaving with cotton, it's a good idea to begin weaving with linen so the fabric won't draw in too much. Weaving a few inches / cm with linen also helps spread the warp ends out evenly from the bunches they are tied in, giving you a beautifully spaced warp in which to weave the "real thing." If your project is in linen or wool, use the same material but in a slightly thicker gauge at the beginning, which will serve the same purpose.

Generally, the shuttle is thrown from the right first. Follow the treadling chart, beginning at the bottom and working up.

Weaving a sample before you start weaving "the real thing" is something I heartily recommend. It's a way to learn about the structure of what you're weaving, and you can also test out different materials and/or colors in the weft. The sample also functions as a kind of "warm-up" for the warp before you start weaving your project. You can use the sample to practice different kinds of finishing, such as braided edges or a special kind of fringe, before using that finishing technique on the bigger piece. Don't forget to add length to the warp for all of the above possibilities.

If the weft is too taut, the fabric will draw in dramatically widthwise, whether or not you use a temple. In each open shed, the weft should run diagonally upward or in a big, soft arc across the warp. This is a matter of dexterity and experience; practice makes perfect. When you change colors or splice the yarn, let the two ends overlap a bit in the same shed.

When the fabric reaches the fabric beam, lay a round of beam sticks between the fabric and the cords, exactly like you did while beaming onto the yarn beam (see page 26) and for the same reason.

TEMPLE OR NO TEMPLE?

Whether or not to use a temple while weaving is a polarizing question, but it can be a very useful tool. A temple holds the fabric at the "correct" width for more even weaving, and also ensures that the selvedge threads don't break due to abrasion by the reed. The temple is measured against the width of the warp in the reed by laying it upside down on top of the warp at the reed. Extend the temple until the selvedge threads are in the middle of the spikes on both sides, and secure that length. The spikes are sharp as needles—it might sound counterintuitive, but that means they go right through the fabric without harming it. Any holes the spikes might leave in the fabric will disappear during the finishing process. After weaving 1½-2 in / 4-5 cm, move the temple, and remove it before you advance the fabric.

TEA TOWELS

There are many ways of weaving these towels. This pattern is for one striped (one color in the weft) and one checked towel (weft uses the same colors as in the warp), and one towel of your choice. If you're going to weave two towels back to back, put a contrasting weft pick between them for easier finishing later.

Technique :	Unbalanced twill, 4 shafts and 4 treadles
Size in loom :	21¼ × 29½ in / 54 × 75 cm per towel
Warp :	Ekelunds organic cotton 8/2 (6,400 m/kg) in orange (225) and ecru (1218)
Weft :	Same yarn as warp
Reed :	12-dent (1 end per heddle, 2 ends per dent) or 50/10, 1-2
Sett :	10 ends per ⅜ in / 1 cm (about 24 epi)
Warp Ends :	540 ends
Width in Reed :	22½ in / 54 cm
Picks :	8 picks per ⅜ in / 1 cm (about 20 ppi)
Warp Order :	By number of ends

ORANGE	ECRU	ORANGE	ECRU	ORANGE	ECRU	ORANGE	ECRU	ORANGE
60	60	60	60	60	60	60	60	60

Threading :	straight draw, see draft on the following page for striped towel, weave 29½ in / 74 cm in ecru
Weaving :	8/2 for checked towel, weave according to the table below:

ORANGE	3½ IN / 9 CM	
ECRU	2½ IN / 6.25 CM	—
ORANGE	2½ IN / 6.25 CM	X4
ECRU	2½ IN / 6.25 CM	—
ORANGE	3½ IN / 9 CM	

Finishing :	Zigzag the short ends and cut apart. Don't forget to add a loop to hang it with if preferred. Wash warm in the machine, line dry, and hem by hand.

DRAFT FOR TEA TOWELS

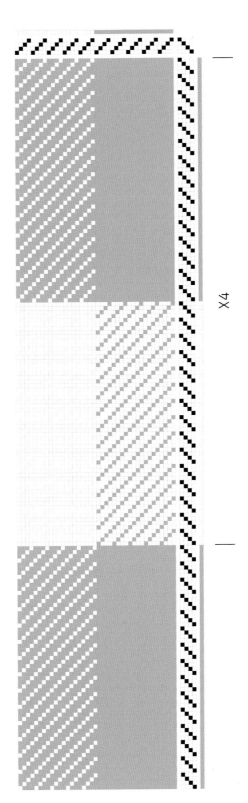

X4

Troubleshooting

One of many good reasons to make a sample at the beginning of your project warp is easy troubleshooting. Weave a few inches or centimeters and analyze the results. Maybe the "problem" is just a function of its handwoven nature? You get to decide if any mistakes you may have made are worth trying to fix. If so, here are a few tips.

THREADING MISTAKES: If you see that the warp and weft ends are not binding as they should, or in one section they don't look the same as in the rest of the weaving, localize the warp ends that you think are causing the problem and check the threading. If the threading is wrong, undo the tie-on; pull the troublesome ends out through the sample, the reed, and the heddles; and re-thread (and re-sley). Then just re-do your tie on. The re-threaded ends will join the weaving after a few weft picks. You may have to tie in a few more heddles to make this work, but if you remove an end from a heddle, the empty heddle can remain throughout the project.

SLEYING MISTAKES: Issues with sleying can be caused by sleying too many ends in a dent or leaving a dent empty by mistake—or maybe both. Unfortunately, sleying issues are often time-consuming to fix. In order for all the ends to be correctly sleyed, in most cases you have to pull out all the ends, from the mistake out to the edge of your warp, and re-sley every one. Choose the closest edge; it doesn't matter which.

A BROKEN WARP END: It's no big deal if a warp end breaks! It happens all the time, especially with thinner or single-ply yarn. Localize the now-empty heddle and identify the corresponding dent. Gently lead the end of the thread that's fixed in the weaving back and out of the way. Put a pin in the fabric horizontally, right under the broken thread, about 1 in / 2.5 cm away from the last weft pick. Measure out a length of the warp yarn 6 in / 15 cm longer than the length of the warp you have left to weave. Wrap one end of that piece of yarn in a figure 8 around the pin and stick the point of the pin into the weaving to fasten it in place. Lead that yarn through the dent and the heddle, and all the way back to your leasing sticks. Find the other end of the original warp thread that broke and tie it together with the new warp end in a bow. You'll untie that bow and move it backward as you move the warp forward. The new warp end will be extremely long, and you can wind it around a bobbin to keep things orderly, if you'd like.

POOR SHED: This often has to do with balance in the loom. The treadles may have been too low when they were tied up, your tie-up cords might be uneven, or your shafts may be sitting too low (your warp ends are at the top of the heddle eye). If your pattern requires many shafts and blocks that are very different sizes (such as for the double weave on page 105), you may need to adjust so that the shafts in back sit slightly higher than those in front.

UNEVEN TENSION: If an end begins to sag a bit during the course of your weaving, there are a few different ways to fix it. You can put a stick between the loose ends and the rest of the warp, on the out-side of the yarn beam. If your warp is very inelastic linen, it's better to put a small butterfly of yarn between the thread and the yarn beam, so that you don't stretch the thread out even more and make the problem worse. You can also hang light weights from the warp, if the material can bear them; this is the best solution for floating selvedges, which almost always end up sagging because they don't bind as tightly as the rest of the warp.

UGLY SELVEDGES: This is partially about dexterity and experience, and it's mostly a question of time and practice! Remember that a lot of "ugliness" will disappear in the wash or during finishing. Aim for equal give in each shuttle throw, and don't pull too hard or jerk the shuttle.

WEFT DOESN'T COVER WARP: For weft-faced techniques such as rölakan, the weft should completely cover the warp. If it doesn't, you may not be making enough arcs across the weft. That is, you're not "feeding" the warp enough weft so that it fills the spaces between warp ends (see the photo on page 71). Maybe you only made three big arcs over the whole width, but you need 10 small arcs to get the right result. If that doesn't help, it may be that the proportions are slightly off, and the sett and the thickness of the weft don't work together. You may have warped too densely for the thickness you want your weft to be. Can you choose a thinner weft? If that doesn't work, a last-ditch effort is to cut every other warp end off for a more open sett.

PRESLEY IS TOO NARROW: Have you calculated your presley in-correctly, and now have to choose between ending up with a nar-rower weaving or redoing the whole thing? The lazy-person solution is to tape a raddle to the back beam and spread the warp out onto the back stick while beaming on. The presleying is always removed, and you'll sley "for real" later in the process anyway.

QUICK TROUBLESHOOTING:

■ "The treadles are locked; I can't press down!"

SOLUTION: Check to see whether the pin holding the top lamms wasn't removed, the cords to the top lamms are twisted, or the treadle cords have tangled. When you're weaving with a ton of shafts and treadles, the cords can sometimes get caught up in each other. If you have metal rods on your treadles, it may be that the wingnut that holds it in place has loosened and the rod is stuck on a cord. Make sure to tighten those wingnuts often.

■ "The shafts are askew, and the warp is lopsided all of a sudden!"

SOLUTION: A shaft may have jumped its hook, or maybe a lamm has become unattached. As soon as anything in the chain of top lamm-shaft-lamm-treadle is wrong, you'll know. Follow that chain from top to bottom, and you'll find the issue.

Now you're equipped to take on our other projects!

Projects

Yardage: Palm Springs

Plain weave may be a simple technique, but it is oh-so-lovely in its simplicity: the meeting of two materials can be enough to create an exciting effect. If you're going to spend the time threading and sleying a big old bunch of tiny threads, you might as well set up a few yards / meters; it takes just as long to set up one yard / meter as it does to set up nine. Yardage in plain weave works up quickly and offers quite a few opportunities for variation and color-and-weave effects. In this yardage project, I mixed linen and cotton in different shades and gauges to maximize the number of different looks I could get out of the same warp, just by changing the weft. Weaving 9 yards / meters of fabric won't get boring when you're constantly trying new combinations. My fabric became a dreamy vacation playset with shorts, top, jacket, and two beach towels, sewn by seamstress Linda Lindgren. But it could also have turned into a skirt, a shirt, palazzo pants, a bunch of hand towels for guests at your cabin—or even a tablecloth!

Technique : Tabby, see page 132 for draft
Size in the loom : 43½ × 355 in (9¾ yd) / 110 cm x 9 m (including loom waste)
Warp : Linen 16/2 (5520 m/kg) and cotton 16/2 (12800 m/kg)
Weft : Linen 16/2 (5520 m/kg), cotton 16/2 (12800 m/kg), cotton 8/2 (6400 m/kg), etc.
Reed : 15-dent (1 end per heddle, 1 ends per dent) or 55/10, 1-1
Sett : 5.5 ends per ⅜ in / 1 cm (about 15 epi)
Warp Ends : 606 ends
Width in Reed : 43½ in / 110 cm
Picks : 9 picks per ⅜ in / 1 cm (about 23 ppi)
Warp Order : Choose your own! My fabric has seven different stripes, either 3 in or 5.5 in / 8 or 14 cm each. A wide multicolored stripe meets a thinner unbleached stripe, which meets a wider single-color stripe, and so on. Warp each stripe separately or split the stripes into three warp chains to be pre-sleyed together into one.
Threading : Straight draw
Weaving : Weave in straight draw treadling. As mentioned in the introduction, the more variation in materials and colors, the better!
Finishing : Zigzag the raw edges and wash the whole fabric in the machine on warm to full the fabric before using. If you're going to sew with this fabric, it's best to stick with straight seams and zigzag. Overlock doesn't suit this open weave.

Placemats & Napkins: Rockport

TEAMWORK — How can you create variation in your weaving without varying your materials? In this project, we have each woven our own set of placemats and napkins; yup, exactly the kind of old-timey project everyone thinks of when you say you're a weaver. Both placemats and napkins are woven in the same warp, for economy and to challenge our design process. Our common denominator is Ekelunds 8/2 cotton, but we chose the colors and technique separately. Are you Team Arianna or Team Miriam, at the dinner table?

ARIANNA'S VERSION: Halvdräll, or simplified overshot, is a brilliant technique that I used to think was way too old-fashioned. I discovered the clean, clear, graphic side of halvdräll though a pattern by the late, great Ylva Kongbäck. And now I'm totally taken by this weave structure. It offers endless combinations of tabby weft, pattern picks, and striped or checked patterning.

Technique:	Halvdräll, a simplified overshot
Size in loom:	Placemats, 14¼ × 18¾ in / 36 × 48 cm; napkins, 14¼ x 12¼ in / 36 × 31 cm
Warp:	Ekelunds organic cotton 8/2 (6,400 m/kg) in light orange 205, light brown 2007, and unbleached
Weft Placemats:	Main/tabby: Ekelunds organic cotton 8/2 (6,400 m/kg) in light orange 205 Pattern: Växbo Lin linen 12/2 (3,600 m/kg), in unbleached and umber
Weft Napkins:	Main/tabby: Ekelunds organic cotton 8/2 (6,400 m/kg) in same colors as warp Pattern: Växbo Lin linen 12/1 (7,200 m/kg) in white, dyed with Levafix (two-color mix: scarlet—brilliant yellow 4:4, strength 0.2%)
Reed:	12-dent (1 end per heddle, 2 ends per dent), or 50/10, 1-2
Sett:	10 ends per ⅜ in / 1 cm (about 24 epi)
Warp Ends:	364
Width in Reed:	14¼ in / 36 cm
Picks:	7 picks per ⅜ in / 1 cm in tabby, 7 main and 6 pattern picks per ⅜ in / 1 cm in pattern (about 17¾ ppi in tabby, 17 main + 16 pattern ppi in pattern)
Threading:	See draft on page 129

Warp order : Follow the table below, in ends:

WHITE		28		28		28		28		28		28	
LIGHT ORANGE	28				28				28					28
LIGHT BROWN			28				28				28		

Weaving, general : Halvdräll is woven on a tabby base, with pattern blocks on single treadles: Block A on Treadle 3 and Block B on Treadle 4. See the draft (page 129) for how to treadle each block. If you're going to weave many in a row, place a contrasting pick between each one to make finishing easier.

Weaving for placemats : Weave 1½ in / 4 cm plain weave, then 15¾ in / 40 cm pattern in Block A, then 1½ in / 4 cm plain weave.

Weaving for napkins : Follow the table on the next page. In the pattern sections, the tabby changes color, but only one pattern weft color is used. It may feel like everything is out of sync, but you can put your faith in the table! It shows the number of picks because I think that's easier to keep track of in the loom when you're working with such small pattern sections.

NUMBER OF PICKS	TABBY COLOR	PATTERN BLOCK
21 PLAIN WEAVE (1¼ IN / 3 CM)	LIGHT ORANGE	PLAIN WEAVE
10 TABBY + 10 PATTERN	LIGHT ORANGE	A
10 TABBY + 10 PATTERN	LIGHT ORANGE	B
10 TABBY + 10 PATTERN	WHITE	B
10 TABBY + 10 PATTERN	WHITE	A
10 TABBY + 10 PATTERN	LIGHT BROWN	A
10 TABBY + 10 PATTERN	LIGHT BROWN	B
10 TABBY + 10 PATTERN	WHITE	B
10 TABBY + 10 PATTERN	WHITE	A
10 TABBY + 10 PATTERN	LIGHT ORANGE	A
10 TABBY + 10 PATTERN	LIGHT ORANGE	B
10 TABBY + 10 PATTERN	WHITE	B
10 TABBY + 10 PATTERN	WHITE	A
10 TABBY + 10 PATTERN	LIGHT BROWN	A
10 TABBY + 10 PATTERN	LIGHT BROWN	B
10 TABBY + 10 PATTERN	WHITE	B
10 TABBY + 10 PATTERN	WHITE	A
10 TABBY + 10 PATTERN	LIGHT ORANGE	A
10 TABBY + 10 PATTERN	LIGHT ORANGE	B
10 TABBY + 10 PATTERN	WHITE	B
10 TABBY + 10 PATTERN	WHITE	A
21 PLAIN WEAVE (1¼ IN / 3 CM)	WHITE	PLAIN WEAVE

Finishing: Zigzag the edges you plan to cut, then cut them apart and wash warm. Dry in the machine or on the line (machine will shrink them more) and hem by hand.

Placemats & Napkins: Oaxaca

MIRIAM'S VERSION: In this warp you could weave placemats and napkins, or lots of napkins and a table runner, or two placemats with the rest for hand towels, or one of each! Using tabby and pointed twill—two easy techniques—in cotton and linen, you can easily change up the pattern, gauge, and feeling.

    After I graduated from Friends of Handicraft in 2016, I worked as a design intern at MZ Fairtrade in Oaxaca, Mexico. I was there from October to December and got to experience the preparations, the parade, and the festivities for *Día de los Muertos*, the Day of the Dead. For this project, I gathered inspiration from the colors, the zigzag patterns, and the raw feeling of experiencing that holiday, when altars decorated with mezcal, gorgeous cobs of corn, and orange, yellow, and pink flowers were everywhere you looked, and the streets echoed with music and cheers from the parades. Smack dab in the middle of all of this, I worked along with many others on our laptops in the town's modern cafés, where the open courtyards offered a cooling respite under the blue sky. In the square, women sat with backstrap looms tensioned against the sycamores' silver-green bark, while I ordered a cappuccino made with local beans or chili-infused hot chocolate served in handmade mugs from the nearby village of Tlacolula. Age-old traditions and youth culture intertwined every day, an environment and a feeling I'll never forget!

Technique : Tabby and pointed twill

Size in loom : Placemats, 13¼ × 16½ in / 33.5 × 42 cm each; napkins, 13¼ × 7¾ in / 33.5 × 20 cm each

Warp : Ekelunds organic cotton 8/2 (6,400 m/kg) in orange 2011 and cherry pink 201, and Växbo Lin 12/2 (3,600 m/kg) in unbleached

Weft : Same as in the warp, plus Ekelunds organic cotton 8/2 (6,400 m/kg) in gray-green 4 and light pink 210

Reed : 12-dent (1 end per heddle, 2 ends per dent), or 45/10, 1-2

Sett : 9 ends per ⅜ in / 1 cm (about 24 epi)

Warp Ends : 304 + 2 extra selvedge ends (threaded and sleyed with the outermost ends on each side) = 306

Width in Reed : 13¼ in / 33.5 cm

Picks : 8 ends per ⅜ in / 1 cm (about 20 ppi)

Warp order : Divided into three chains:
1st chain:
9 ends cherry pink 201
9 ends orange 2011
2nd chain:
266 ends linen 12/2, unbleached
3rd chain:
9 ends orange 2011
9 ends cherry pink 201

These are presleyed together into one warp, with the cherry pink sections at the selvedges.

Threading : Pointed twill, see the draft on page 128.

Weaving, General : Tie up the twill on page 128 and 2 tabby treadles. Each piece begins and ends with about 2 in / 5 cm of tightly woven tabby (which will need more treadles) in cotton 8/2 for hemming and as a contrasting edge.

Weaving, Placemats : Between the hems described above, weave with cotton 8/2 wound double, in pointed twill as shown in the draft on page 128.

Weaving, Napkins : Between the hems described above, you can play around with surfaces and stripes with all the given colors. Maybe single-wound cotton in tabby, or double-wound linen in twill, or stripes of both? Test out different variations!

Finishing : Soak the whole piece of fabric, then wash in a machine on hot. Try not to scrunch up the fabric; place it in the machine like an accordion so it can move freely while washing. Let air dry, and then cut into separate pieces. Use a spray bottle to dampen each piece and iron it flat. Fold in a double hem and sew with a straight seam on a machine or by hand. The napkins can be finished with only a zigzag stitch on a raw edge or machine hemmed.

Rölakan: Technique

Rölakan is a flatweave technique in which the weft is picked up by hand instead of thrown with a shuttle. You use your hands directly in the warp and handle many wefts at a time across the width of the same open shed. The design can be geometrically perfect with exacting, calculated shapes, or intentionally unplanned. Countless effects can be created by varying the weft yarns and colors.

Rölakan is an age-old technique with its lineage and heritage extending back to humanity's earliest civilizations. The name is probably derived from the Swedish word *rygglakan*, which is the term for the kind of traditional wall hangings that insulated log cabins from the cold winds that could squeeze in between the timbers and chill your spine. Surviving examples of rugs and carriage cushions from the 18th and 19th centuries, with advanced, detailed designs in rölakan, come mostly from southern and southwestern Sweden, but also from a few other areas across the country. In Oaxaca, they looked at me quizzically when I asked what the name of this technique is in Spanish; there, it's just called *la tecnica*, "the technique." However, during my internship, it was enormously helpful for me to be able to share some of my rölakan samples from school—the things I couldn't yet communicate in Spanish, I could communicate through weaving.

I love rölakan and am especially inspired by both carriage cushions from Skåne in "lightning rölakan," and North American "eye-dazzlers." More examples can be found in the Middle East and northern Africa. It's fascinating how the same technique can be a foundation for such broad variation in design, and at the same time so clearly belong to the same group.

TECHNIQUE

Rölakan can be woven in squares or in diagonals. I work mostly in diagonal rölakan, which is built on the principle that you advance every weft at least one warp end in one shed, and in the next shed only go back as far as the neighboring weft advanced. This creates a gradual progression in the form of a diagonal. A weaving with a turquoise background and a pattern in yellow would require three wefts (made into so-called "butterflies") in each shed: a turquoise butterfly on either side of the yellow. As long as the three butterflies are moved in the same direction in that one shed, the yellow line shifts through the turquoise area. When you suddenly change directions—that is, advance the wefts one warp end further in the opposite shed—the line is broken and a lightning bolt or a zigzag starts to take shape.

RHOMBUS

A rhombus begins as a tiny point in one lowered and one raised warp end, with two other butterflies to either side of it. The butterfly that builds the rhombus moves back and forth and constantly advances over a new warp end in each shed. The butterflies on either side "meet" the rhombus further and further away from the center. For a rhombus with multiple colors, each new color is placed in the center of the existing rhombus in the same way. Like rings on water, the number of butterflies on each side of the rhombus' center grows with each color you add. When the rhombus is as wide as you'd like, you change direction and the side-butterflies "come back" to the center, advancing one warp end back over the rhombus, which closes gradually with every weft row.

TRIANGLE

To make a triangle, you begin the opposite way. Instead of just the point, the entire breadth of the triangle should be laid in at the beginning. For example, for a triangle that is 2½ in / 5 cm wide, the first weft should be laid over the equivalent of 2½ in / 5 cm in the warp. The butterflies on either side then advance 1 warp end in over the triangle to gradually reduce its width, forming the diagonal triangle sides that eventually meet at the point and close the triangle.

In the beginning, it can be difficult to keep track of when to move and when not to, but it will be clear when something's gone wrong, and in that case all you have to do is back up and remove a few weft rows. Once you've gotten the hang of the proportions and construction, you can start experimenting: all forms more or less start with the rhombus, the triangle, or the lightning. Variations can build on:

PLACEMENT: Forms can be woven together in a border over the entire warp width or separated from each other with a background color in between.

PROGRESSION: The weft can move over 1 or more warp ends at a time. They can also move in both directions—for example, 2 warp ends in one direction and 1 warp end in the other direction.

HALF-SHAPES/MIRRORING: A triangle can become a rhombus and

then become a triangle again. Lightning zigs and zags can be in the same row but in different directions—one advances one warp end while the other goes "back."

COLOR CHOICE: Never underestimate a color effect!

HOW TO MAKE A BUTTERFLY

When I make butterflies, I hold one hand like a "pistol." Begin by putting one end of the yarn(s) in the palm of your hand so it comes down between your finger and thumb and ends at your pinky finger. Close your pinky, ring, and middle fingers around the yarn and hold on. Wrap the yarn in a figure 8 around your pointer finger and thumb; the number of wraps that will fit depends on the gauge of your yarn and how many strands you're using. Cut the yarn about 6 in / 15 cm away from the butterfly and wrap it widthwise around that pointer-thumb figure 8 so it becomes more like a bow. Tuck that end into the wraps, but leave the other starting end free. That's the end you'll weave with.

REMEMBER:

- For an even, flat result, you'll need to use the same yarn or yarns of similar gauge. Different gauge yarns will build up differently and make crooked lines.

- In a new shed, always begin with the same butterfly you ended with in the previous shed, you should be traveling back and forth across the warp.

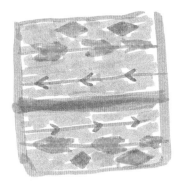

Try sketching both straight and curvy shapes that you can then translate into rölakan weavings.

These butterflies are secured in an open shed to start a border with arrows that will be pointing two different ways. In the beginning, they're only half the shape of an arrow—that is, they look like parallelograms. There will also be a yellow rhombus in the middle; notice how the yellow butterfly is only laid over one lowered and one raised warp end.

Here you can see how the arrows on the left side advance one warp end over the next color, while the ones on the right do not. In the next shed (that is, when you've treadled the other treadle and opened the second plain weave shed), the opposite is true: the arrows on the right side advance toward the rhombus, and the left arrows do not. In the middle of the yellow rhombus, I've now added another color: a pink butterfly is secured in the same way the yellow one was in the beginning, and I've added an extra yellow butterfly next to the pink one to continue the rhombus.

Now the arrows have assumed their characteristic shape. When the arrow is
exactly half as big as you'd like it to be, switch directions and begin
to advance the opposite direction to build up the other half. The rhombus
has also reversed. Notice how my hand is truly IN the warp; this is what
is meant by "picking up" the weft instead of throwing the shuttle.

DECORATIVE BORDERS

A common accompaniment to rölakan weaving is a shuttle-thrown
border, perfect for beginning and ending your weaving. By using
different colors in different orders, you can create a range of patterns. For example, *"dientes,"* a border pattern named for the vertical "teeth" that are created by throwing alternating picks of two
different colors. In Sweden, these are often called *staplar* ("piles"),
but I think the Mexican term is much more fun. In the photos, the
dientes border is furthest down, in turquoise and yellow. Above that,
I've thrown in other variations—for example, two picks of brown and
then two picks of yellow for horizontal stripes (furthest up). Try it
yourself; what happens when you mix two different colors in different orders?

Rölakan: Projects

PILLOWS

Technique :	Rölakan, a weft-faced plain weave
Finished Sizes :	Pillows that are 24 × 24 in / 60 × 60 cm and 24 × 12 in / 60 × 30 cm.
Size in loom :	24½ × 25½ in / 62 × 65 cm and 24½ × 13¾ in / 62 × 35 cm
Warp :	Holma Helsinglands Möbelåtta 8/2 (4,000 m/kg) in white
Weft :	Wool rug yarn 1.3/1 (1,300 m/kg) in various colors
Reed :	9-dent (1 end per heddle, 1 end per dent) or 35/10, 1-1
Sett :	3.5 ends per ⅜ in / 1 cm (about 9 epi)
Ends :	218 + 4 selvedge ends (threaded and sleyed double on either selvedge) = 222
Width :	24½ in / 62 cm
Threading :	Straight draw

WEAVING: Straight draw in plain weave. Begin and end each weaving with a 1 in / 2.5 cm hem/seam allowance in a thinner yarn. Leave 3¼ in / 8 cm between each weaving for finishing; you can weave with rag scraps or place sticks in between. Otherwise, you can weave all of them together in one piece, and zigzag carefully and well on each edge before cutting apart.

FINISHING: If you've left space between the pieces, you can tie together the warp ends, two and two, on both edges (although this usually isn't necessary with a wide enough seam allowance. Wash them in lukewarm water from the tap and air-dry flat. Press with an iron and sew together with your choice of backing into a pillow. Don't trim the corners on the inside (as you might normally); the weaving will unravel. Pressing properly will give you nice, rounded corners.

REMEMBER:

■ The first weaving you do in a fresh warp should be woven with a shuttle. If you begin the pick-up immediately and start pulling on the warp ends to create your pattern, the tension can quickly become uneven. If you make a mirrored form, remember that the upper section will look taller than the first half because it hasn't been packed together as much yet. It's easy to think you've done something wrong, but don't worry!

RUG

Here, it's up to you to decide the measurements of the rug.
Warp : Holma-Helsingland linen rug warp 8/5 (1000 m/kg) in unbleached
Reed : 5-dent (1 end per heddle, 1 end per dent) or 20/10, 1-2
Sett : 4 ends per ⅜ in / 1 cm (10 epi), but see description below

For a strong and tightly woven rug, 3-6 strands of yarn are often used in each butterfly. This can also make it easy to create dynamic color blends and gradations. The sett is more open than with the pillows, in order to allow the warp to "accept" the thicker weft without showing. Warping with 1 end in each heddle as you thread and 2 in each dent as you sley makes it easier to secure the ends of the butterflies; with 5 epi (2 epcm), it would be impossible.

BILDVÄV ("PICTURE-WEAVING," OR TAPESTRY WEAVING), METHOD 1

Bildväv, or "picture-weaving," is the Swedish word for what many call tapestry weaving. In tapestry weaving, you can build up shapes without ever using the beater. Instead, you use your fingers, the side of your hand, or a range of different tools to shape and pack the warp into the weft. You will often be working on one form at a time. While in rölakan you are building across the entire width of the warp in each shed, in tapestry you might change sheds many times while only building up one section of the warp.

In a "free tapestry," you literally choose freely between different techniques to achieve your desired result. You might use reversible (Norwegian) rölakan (advance in one direction, back the other way), interlocking weft rölakan (the wefts interlock with each other in the same shed without locking around a warp end), or kilim (two wefts each lock around neighboring warp ends when they "meet," and create a vertical hole/slit).

It took a long time for me to understand how this could work. Aren't the warp ends "closed off" where you've built up the weft, with an inaccessible hole next to them? Sure, a hole will be created if you repeatedly turn on the same warp end and don't move on to an adjacent end; that's how you make a kilim slit. This is a technique in and of itself and can create a whole new pattern of light coming through the slits. If you don't want kilim slits, you have to remember to work a little at a time when you're building up your shapes. If you want a tall, thin shape in the middle, you can't just build the entire length of it at once. If you do, the warp ends on either edge of that shape will be closed off, and only accessible way too far up in the warp to be connected with the shapes on either side. Instead, you should weave and build it up gradually, and make sure that the weft from that shape also overlaps the warp ends of its neighbor shapes.

BILDVÄV ("PICTURE-WEAVING," OR TAPESTRY WEAVING), METHOD 2

A quick and easy tapestry weave can be created by mixing together different weft gauges. Using randomly chosen colors, you can make a multicolored surface resembling a rolling landscape emerge, even though you're using the beater.

Choose a color scale in various types of yarn (though all the same material): soft-spun/hard-spun, matte/shiny, single-ply/multi-ply. You may want to begin by using the shuttle to weave a foundation. Make single-strand butterflies of each of the yarns and place them in the shed at irregular intervals (don't count warp ends; let the width of each form be random). Start to move in one direction, and begin to create a diagonal. After a few weft picks, change direction. Or cut off all the butterflies, bury the ends, and begin again. Secure each new butterfly in a different, random place in the warp. Weave one round of wide shapes, and then make the next round thin. If a butterfly runs out, start with a new color in its place. Weave one round with only a few butterflies (a few colors), then one round with many (lots of different colors). By randomly mixing different areas of color and types of yarn, you end up with different surfaces and structures, making the weaving lively and uneven—round shapes can emerge even though you're beating after every weft.

Scratch paper with mountain silhouettes, painted with pigment from a handful of dirt saved from a New Mexico roadtrip in 2018. The blue section is from the dyeing you can see on page 120—here I was testing how the color would look.

A rölakan weaving works beautifully sewn into a laptop case.

Shuttle-Woven Pillow

TEAMWORK — What happens with a weaving project if two people each have a say in the process? In this project, Arianna chose a weave structure that Miriam rarely uses, and Miriam dyed the warp in a colorway that Arianna would never have chosen. The result is a great example of how much each person can affect the outcome, and it turns out that it can be fun and surprising to work outside your usual frame of reference. These patterns are for pillows that measure 20 × 20 in / 50 × 50 cm when finished.

ARIANNA: This technique is called *droppdräll*, or huckaback, and is traditionally used in a much thinner execution for carefully pressed tablecloths and napkins. But in one of my vintage weaving books, Maja Lundbäck uses what is supposed to be the fabric's "back side" with much thicker yarns in the pattern picks to create a really interesting upholstery fabric. I was taken with this slightly unhinged version of such a dainty technique, and I've used it for everything from pillows to beach towels. The take-up in the warp is dramatic, so I always weave a bit of extra plain weave on either end of pillows in this technique to make sure that there is sufficient fabric to sew with.

MIRIAM: I dyed the warp before weaving to add an abstract color effect to the more rhythmic woven pattern. I made two warp chains, both snugly tied off in a few extra places before being removed from the mill. The dyeing was done with the help of many small dyebaths in different shades of the same base color. The warp chains, which can be soaked beforehand for softer gradations or kept dry for sharper contrasts, were then dipped like a long snake into the baths and dyed according to my instructions on page 121. Graphic vertical color transitions were created when the two chains were beamed on and the different colors of each chain met in the center. Horizontal patterns appeared like radio waves where the warp was tied off during the dyeing process.

Technique :	*Droppdräll* (huckaback) variation
Size in loom :	ARIANNA: 21½ × 24½ in / 55 × 62 cm
	MIRIAM: 21½ × 21½ in / 55 × 55 cm
Warp :	Möbelåtta 8/2 (4,000 m/kg) in white, dyed according to the text above
Weft :	ARIANNA, tabby: Ekenäs Hantverk Gotland wool singles (4,200 m/kg) in gray; pattern: Båvens corespun wool rug yarn (100 m/kg) in white
	MIRIAM, tabby: two-ply wool yarn (probably 3,000 m/kg), dyed yellow-green; pattern: Lankava wool yarn 2.5/6 (400 m/kg) and same two-ply as in tabby, both dyed yellow-green
Reed :	10-dent (1 end per heddle, 2 ends per dent), or
Sett :	40/10, 1-2
Ends :	8 ends per ⅜ in / 1 cm (about 20 epi)
Width in Reed :	440
Picks :	21½ in / 55 cm
	6 ends per ⅜ in / 1 cm in plain weave (about 15 epi)
Threading :	see the draft on page 133

WEAVING: In Swedish drafts, thicker weft picks are drawn as two picks on top of each other in the draft. That doesn't mean that you should weave two picks, it's simply to show the difference in thicknesses in the drawdown. Block A is on Treadle 1, Block B is on Treadle 4. When you are weaving with staggered dots, you need an even number of tabby picks in between, and when you're weaving with dots in a vertical line, you need an uneven number of tabby picks in between.

WEAVING FOR ARIANNA'S VERSION

I wanted to max out the size difference between the tabby and the pattern picks. The yarns I chose are both wool yarns from small Swedish businesses, Ekenäs Hantverk and Båvens Spinnery. The thick wool rug yarn from Båvens takes up so much space in the warp that it almost looks like it's trying to escape. Using extremely thick weft means that there is a ton of warp take-up, which I've accounted for in the length of the pillow in the loom. Follow the table below:

PLAIN WEAVE/TABBY	PATTERN AND BLOCK
4 IN / 10 CM	
	2 IN / 5 CM, A-B-A-B
1¼ IN / 3 CM	
	2½ IN / 6 CM, BLOCK B ONLY
1¼ IN / 3 CM	
	3 IN / 8 CM, B-A-B-A-B-A
1¼ IN / 3 CM	
	2½ IN / 6 CM, BLOCK A ONLY
1¼ IN / 3 CM	
	2 IN / 5 CM, B-A-B-A
4 IN / 10 CM	

WEAVING FOR MIRIAM'S VERSION

I used the same color throughout in the weft, a yellow-green in both the thin and the thicker picks. Additional color variation comes from the dyed warp.

PLAIN WEAVE/ TABBY	PATTERN AND BLOCK
8½ IN / 22 CM	3 IN / 8 CM WITH TABBY YARN IN BOTH TABBY AND PATTERN, BLOCKS A & B
	6 IN / 15 CM WITH THICK YARN IN EVERY OTHER PATTERN PICK, BLOCKS A & B
	4 IN / 10 CM WITH TABBY YARN IN BOTH TABBY AND PATTERN, BLOCKS A & B

FINISHING: Zigzag the raw edges and sew into a pillow 20 × 20 in / 50 × 50 cm using your choice of technique. See Miriam's finishing description for her rya cushion on page 74 for an envelope closure cushion.

Rya: Technique

A rya is a textile that has a tabby base and knots on top. *Nockor* is what the knots are called in Swedish, and they form a pile or fringe of yarn that can be long or short, but that is always longer and sparser than its tight, short cousin, flossa. Rya can be worked on a loom, sewn with a needle in a premade fabric base, or made with a tufting gun that shoots yarn into a premade backing. Rya weaves have a long history in Sweden and have functioned as comforters on beds (*slitrya* or *båtrya*), as decorative insulation on the wall, and as one of the trendiest interior design objects of the middle of the 20th century.

From the 1950s to the 1970s, rya weaves were extremely popular, and there was an abundance of ready-made DIY kits for sale where you followed a pattern drawn by a famous designer. I've heard countless tales of how young couples used to sit in front of the fire in their rec room and work on a rya weave together. My dream scenario can be found in a 1966 article in *Life* on "The Modern Craftsman." Photographer Nina Leens' images illustrate weaving's new popularity with a portrait of a young woman, wearing short black high-waisted shorts and a yellow top, sitting and working on a rya weaving in a green landscape that must be somewhere in California. The rya project she's working on looks like a deep blue or light purple flower bed in the middle of all that green, or a magic carpet of moss. The whole thing looks like it could just as well have been published today.

Despite that dreamy vision, I've still never made a rya weave on a premade base; the loom offers much more freedom, greater ability to choose, and better quality. Any image, feeling, structure, or shape can grow out of woven rya's tabby base. The freedom is in your hands.

The construction of rya is easiest to explain in terms of beads or pixels: every knot is one pixel, one bead. An image or motif is built up row by row, as on a perler board, and the more pixels you have per row, the clearer the picture—just like with digital photos, where higher resolution makes for a sharper picture and lower resolution, a blurrier one. Different thicknesses and types of yarn contribute a great deal of feeling to rya. A lighter section in the middle of a dark area can be accentuated by using a thinner yarn there, to contrast with the thicker, darker yarn surrounding it. The light section may even have shorter pile than the darker area, which creates even more depth and dimension. Because each knot in rya consists of a combination of yarns—a butterfly—the possibilities are endless for blending colors and tonalities.

In the following three project descriptions, I explain how I make rya pieces in three different ways. Knotting freely with stash yarn and geometric shapes for a cushion; following a sketch on graph paper for classic "floor rya"; and how to translate freely from a sketch to make a larger *slitrya* blanket.

1. The butterfly is passed under one warp end.

2. The butterfly is passed over to the next warp end, then under that second end to make the knot.

3. The length of the pile is measured and maintained with your choice of method; here, I'm using my fingers. Pull hard on the knot.

4. When the whole row is knotted, make arcs with the tabby weft: first small arcs, then smaller as you see in the photo. The selvedge yarn is woven only on the outer two pairs of ends. The tabby weft interlocks with the nearest sel-vedge warp ends every other pick to bind the edge and the weaving together.

Rya Cushion: Årsta

This project is a good introduction to rya, perfect for understanding the framing and construction, and at the same time it doesn't take too long before it "becomes something." The shape is determined by the yarn you have on hand; choose a color combination you like, and see how much yarn you can gather in those tones. The more yarn you have, the bigger the pillow or cushion can be. The more consistent the yarn gauge, the more even the surface. Soft-spun yarns (think: fluffier) make for a smooth, soft surface while hard-spun yarns are a bit crinklier. I like to mix the two. This pillow gets its abstract feeling from Årsta's 1950s architecture and the art in Årsta Square that I pass by every day on the way to the studio, with a little splash of brick red tow linen. For more on my sketching process, see the chapter on Design Process (page 109).

Technique : Rya with a tabby base
Size in loom : 34½ × 18¾ in / 86 × 48 cm
Warp : Holma-Helsingland linen rug warp 8/5 (1,000 m/kg)
Weft : Tabby, wool singles, e.g., wool rug yarn 1.3/1 (1,300 m/kg) or a soft-spun 2-ply yarn; pile, many strands of wool and linen yarn, varied. See note above.
Reed : 8-dent (1 end per heddle and 1 end per dent), or 30/10, 1-1

I needed about 400 g of yarn for the tabby base and about 400 g total for the knots/pile.

Sett : 3 ends per ⅜ in / 1 cm (about 8 epi)
Ends : 264 + 2 extra selvedge ends that are threaded and sleyed with the outermost warp ends = 266
Width in Reed : 34½ in / 86 cm
Threading : Straight draw

WEAVING: First, weave a hem/selvedge 1½ in / 4 cm long in plain weave. In a neutral shed (no treadles lowered), pick up a pair of warp ends ¾ in / 2 cm from the edge; these will be your first knot of your first row. Choose the length of your pile. I often knot around my ring and pinky fingers to get a pile length of about 1 in / 2.5 cm. Hop over 2 warp ends and tie the next knot. Continue with the same butterfly/color, or switch when you want to begin a new shape, until ¾ in / 2 cm remain of the warp width. Open the shed again and weave about ½ in / 1.2 cm. For your first 2-3 tabby weft picks, you should make many small arcs (see page 71) over the knot row, so that the weft really covers the knots and creates a tightly woven surface. Use a temple if you need to in order to keep from drawing in. When all the tabby picks are in place, remove the temple (if using) and cut up your loops into pile. Begin the next row. Finish with 1½ in / 4 cm of hem/selvedge in plain weave.

FINISHING: Make sure to leave unwoven warp when you cut down for finishing. Tie the warp ends together two and two with overhand knots on both ends of the weaving. Then cut them short. Choose a fabric for the back side—for example, a thick cotton or a wool felt—and sew a pillow using your choice of technique. I usually sew them on a machine with a jeans needle, with the backing fabric overlapped so that it becomes a "pocket" on the back side to slide the pillow into; this is sometimes called an "envelope" closure. Sew with about ½ in / 1 cm seam allowance on the short sides and ¾ in / 2 cm on the long sides. It may feel difficult to keep your seams straight on a machine with such thick and somewhat unruly fabric. But the thick fabric is also what makes this project forgiving, so if you think you've gone astray, turn the pillowcase right side out first and see how it looks before ripping out your seams and starting over. Don't clip your corners on the inside; pressing them vigorously with an iron on the outside should do the trick for nice, rounded corners.

REMEMBER:

■ There is nothing wrong with making big sections in just one color! It may seem boring or too rational to knot a large shape in only one color, but it's actually quite a powerful aesthetic.

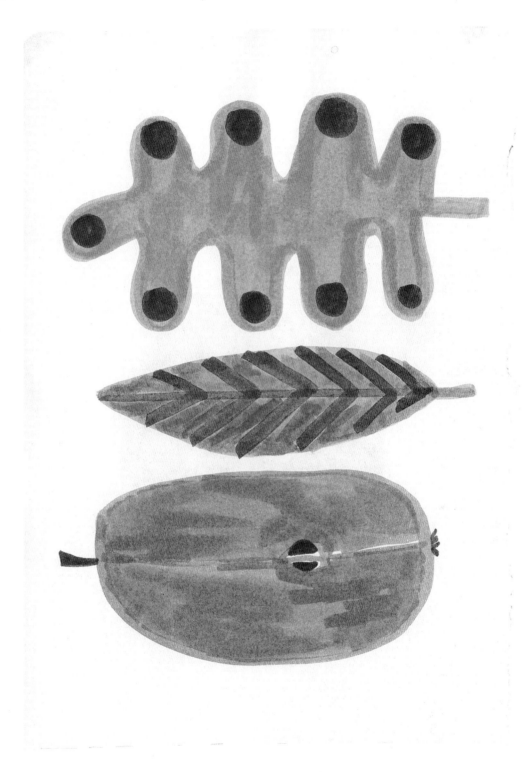

Color sketch for a classic rya carpet. The description is on the next page.

Classic Rya Carpet: Folio Room

With all due respect to the unplanned, the free, and the improvised, here is a project that you can follow from the first warp thread to the last knot! It's a relatively easy sketch to follow for those of you who are new to weaving, with room for variation and change for those who want to. The borders can easily be re-drawn due to their geometric formation; the border colors can be switched around and every field can be given more pattern by weaving stripes, polka-dots, or smaller squares. For the pear and the two leaves in the middle, you can choose how you want to interpret the colors in the sketch and compose your color blends. And remember! Rya takes a lot of time. It will take longer than you think. But it's worth it, I promise!

Technique : Rya with a tabby base
Size in loom : 31½ × 44½ in / 80 × 113 cm
Warp : Rauma Åkle wool yarn (1,750 m/kg) in white 701
Weft : Tabby, Rauma Åkle wool yarn (1,750 m/kg) in white 701; edge, Rauma ullspissgarn (1,300 m/kg) in white 901; pile, Rauma Åkle wool yarn (1,750 m/kg) and Rye yarn (750 m/kg) in various colors (see table below)
Reed : 8-dent (1 end per heddle and 1 end per dent), or 30/10, 1-1
Sett : 3 ends per ⅜ in / 1 cm (about 8 epi)
Ends : 240 + 4 selvedge ends (2 per heddle and 2 per dent x 2 on each side) = 244
Width in Reed : 31½ in / 80 cm
Threading : straight draw

CORAL/PINK	BROWN	LIGHT BLUE/PETROL
RYE 562 (200 G)	RYE 581 (300 G)	RYE 521 (300 G)
ÅKLE 739 (200 G)		ÅKLE 754 (200 G)
YELLOW-GREEN/OCHRE	WHITE	
RYE 531 (200 G)	RYE 501 (600 G)	
ÅKLE 746 (200 G)		

WEAVING: Begin with a sample if you want to test something out before you begin the "real" weaving. Weave with rags or a similar material for about 4 in / 10 cm, in order to leave warp to make an edge or fringe. Begin with 2 in / 5 cm of *dientes* (see page 57). I chose stripes of yellow and blue Åkle yarn for the first edge, and pink and blue Åkle on the other.

Then weave ¾ in / 2 cm of white Åkle in plain weave; this will be used for the tabby as well. Add the edge butterflies, which are composed of two strands of white wool rug yarn. These run back and forth over only the outermost doubled warp ends (selvedges). Every other tabby pick, the shuttle also winds around the nearest doubled selvedge and binds the edge to the weaving. Each pattern butterfly has two strands: a mix of two different colors and/or types of yarn, or two of the same. The knot rows are made in a neutral shed (no treadle lowered) and begin on the first warp end pair after the selvedges, with one warp end skipped between each knot. I knot around my pinky and ring fingers, as seen on page 71, but a piece of cardboard in the right width can also be used (like a flossa ruler). When a row is fully knotted, weave 8 tabby picks (remember to interlock the edges). Before the next knot row is begun, cut the pile loops. When all the rows are knotted, weave ½ in / 1 cm white Åkle in plain weave and then another decorative *dientes* border.

FINISHING: Tie all the warp ends together two and two with an overhand knot. Make an "oriental braid" with four pairs of warp ends, starting by laying the rug face down on a table with a weight on top to hold it in place. Begin on the left hand side, holding the first 8 warp ends (in four pairs) taut in your hand. Think of it as making a plain weave shed: the first pair is down, the second pair is up, the third down and the fourth up. Pull the first pair through the "shed" and lay it up on top of the rug under the weight. Now you have three pairs left in your hand. Pick up the next pair to the right so that you have four pairs again and repeat the last step: the first pair goes through the "shed" and is laid on top of the rug.

Eventually you may need to adjust the "finished" braided pairs to achieve an even and handsome braid. This technique both binds the ends and makes for a clean finish. When you've braided the entire edge, you end up with 5 pairs; braid these together in a four-strand braid. All the ends that have just been folded upward are turned outward again by braiding them together in groups of three pairs, making a fringe. Secure each one with an overhand knot and cut the ends to your preferred length.

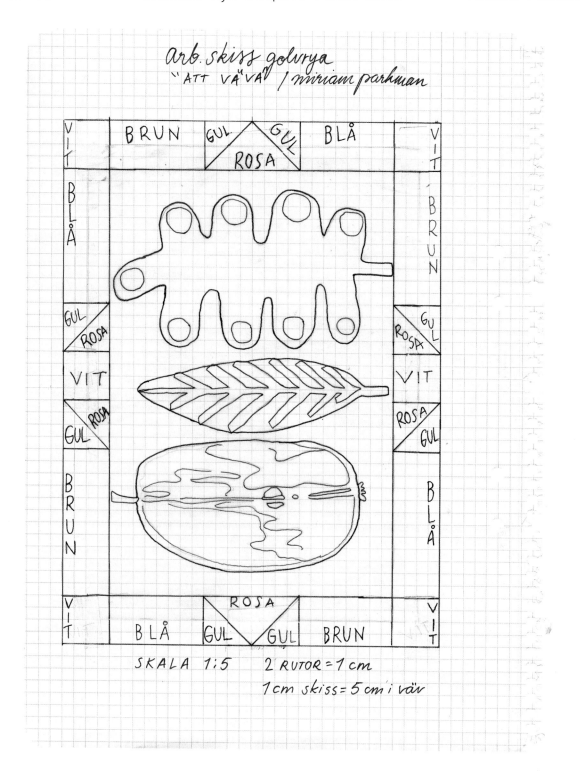

arb. skiss golvrya
"ATT VÄVA" / miriam parkman

SKALA 1:5   2 RUTOR = 1 cm
1 cm skiss = 5 cm i väv

Note that the sketch (labeled in Swedish) was originally done on size A4 paper.

Slitrya Blanket

Compared to rya carpets, *slitrya* are soft. They aren't beaten as hard, and therefore have a soft, blanketlike feeling. Luxurious! For this project you're going to make your own sketch. Read more about how I made my sketch, and get inspired to make your own, on page 116. I always begin and end my *slitrya* blankets with a rölakan edge. Read more about that technique on page 53.

Technique : *Slitrya* with a tabby base
Size in loom : Mine was 36¼ × 88½ in / 92 × 225 cm, but yours can be any size
Warp : Möbelåtta (4,000 m/kg) in white
Weft : Tabby, same as in warp or slightly thicker, soft 2-ply wool; pile, different wool yarns: thin and thick, hard-spun and soft-spun, singles and multi-ply
Reed : 9-dent (1 end per heddle and 1 end per dent), or 35/10, 1-1
Sett : 3.5 ends per ⅜ in / 1 cm (about 9 epi)
Ends : 322 + 2 selvedge ends (2 ends per heddle and 2 ends per dent x 1 each side) = 324
Width in Reed : 36¼ in / 92 cm

HOW TO CALCULATE MATERIAL NEEDED FOR A RYA:

My most common unit of measurement is 1 knot per ⅜ in / 1 cm, ⅜ in / 1 cm between each knot, and ⅜ in / 1 cm tabby (including the knot row).

Calculate the number of knots per row using this formula:
Number of ends / sett in cm / 2 = number of knots per row

In this case:
324 ends / 3.5 = 92.57, rounded to 92 for an even number
92 / 2 = 46 knots per row

How much material is needed for each knot depends on how long and dense your pile is. Four strands in a butterfly become 8 strands in a knot. Maybe 2 strands in each butterfly is enough, which gives you 4 strands in each knot. Remember that you can choose the number of strands in each knot as you go along, but in order to calculate how much material you're going to need (for effective purchasing and in case you'd like to dye), we are considering all knots equal.

46 knots x 2 strands x 1.5 in / 4 cm per knot = 145 in (4 yd) / 368 cm (3.68 m) of yarn per knot row. Depending on which yarns you use, you can calculate how many rows you can get out of a skein, and then calculate how many skeins or grams/oz are needed for each color.

Example:
Yarns have a m/kg measurement that is given on the label or a company's website. For example, 2,100 m/kg. A skein is often 100 g, which means a skein in this case would contain 210 m of yarn. 210 m total / 3.68 m per row = 57. That is, a skein of yarn with this m/kg measurement would be enough for 57 rows of knots.

GENERAL: I'm bad at math, and on top of that I prefer not to have everything decided beforehand. Therefore, I always begin by making the calculations above to get a sense of how much yarn I'll need. But I also always add some extra length onto every warp and dye more yarn than I'll need. That allows me to be flexible, and also covers for any mistakes along the way. Extra yarn from one project will always find a place in another—especially with rya. Mixing different gauges and types of yarn gives the pieces a livelier look, and even a little snippet, just 1.5 in / 4 cm long, can be useful somewhere!

WEAVING: Use the same process as for the earlier rya projects, but remember to NOT beat too hard. When you weave the tabby picks between the knot rows, the warp should NOT be totally covered in this case, in order to give the piece its characteristic flowing appearance.

FINISHING: "Oriental braid", sewn hem (weave at least 2¾ in / 7 cm of plain weave, and fold in twice to make a hem), or simply braided or twisted fringe. A sewn hem can also be reinforced with an additional sewn edge—for example, soft leather, or another type of fabric.

RYA "Hemma igen"
3 månader Oaxaca

A watercolor sketch of wintery blue mountains in Nordingrå, Sweden was the model
for my *slitrya* blanket.

Flossa: Technique

Flossa is my very favorite technique. As soon as I started school at Friends of Handicraft, I knew I wanted to try to get my Journeyman Certification at the end of my time there. In the first year of the Advanced Textile Course, you get to try out weaving rugs. That was when I discovered the technique I would later use to weave my journeyman project: flossa. The technique is very similar to rya; it even uses the same kind of knot. But flossa is much denser, and the pile is much shorter.

Linen warp is very interesting to work with. It's inelastic and difficult to beam on evenly, but it's an excellent foundation for a sturdy and stable rug. When you beam on, you should have help from at least two good friends with strong hands and a lot of patience. For the best results, add at least a meter or yard to the warp so the back stick stays on the yarn beam throughout the weaving. Weave a generous sample at the beginning, enough that the front stick is past the breast beam before you begin the "real" weaving. This isn't strictly necessary, but it's a journeyman tip that I think it's important to share. By the way, I got my certification—and a large medal of honor and a fanfare from the Police Music Corps at the ceremony!

When you sketch for flossa, you can begin with graph paper, or sketch in your choice of technique and lay a grid over it. This technique is quite pixelated on paper, and I like to take advantage of that quality in my designs. But your sketch can absolutely be figural or flowing also. For this piece, I used the relationship between the size and sett/picks per inch or cm that we learned at Friends of Handicraft School: using 3 ends per ⅜ in / 1 cm in the warp (about 8 epi), you get 15 knots per 4 in / 10 cm across the width, and you want the same lengthwise in the warp. To get 15 knots per 4 in / 10 cm lengthwise, your knot row and tabby picks should measure slightly longer than ¼ in / 0.66 cm together. This may seem like an annoyingly specific measurement, but it's a good starting point. You can also just measure every tenth or fifteenth row: 10 rows = 2½ in / 6.6 cm, 15 rows = 4 in / 10 cm, 30 rows = 7¾ in / 20 cm, etc. Adjust the number of tabby rows as needed to increase or decrease the length of each row and maintain the correct proportions in your design. You can use whatever yarns you'd like in the knots, but don't use too much. Flossa is so dense that there's a risk that the knots will take up too much space widthwise. That makes it hard to beat the row to ¼ in / 0.66 cm, and if you can't achieve that number, the finished piece won't lie flat.

SPECIAL TOOLS

FLOSSA RULER: You can make flossa pile loops in many ways—around your pinky finger, for example—but it's well worth it to invest in a flossa ruler. Your results will be more even and it's more efficient (read: you weave faster!) With a flossa ruler, loops can slashed instead of cut; a whole row of 150 loops can become pile in 5 seconds flat.

FLOSSA KNIFE/BOX CUTTER: A flossa knife has a shield on one side of the blade that keeps the blade from getting too close to the warp. A box cutter is a cheaper alternative and is also easier to find. If you use a box cutter, I suggest you cover the warp with a quilting mat. I've accidentally cut off many warp ends, and it's a royal pain.

Flossa Rug

Technique : Flossa on a tabby base
Size in loom : 22½ × 16 in / 57 × 40 cm
Warp : Holma-Helsingland linen warp 8/5 (950 m/kg)
Weft : Tabby, Rauma ullspiss yarn (1,300 m/kg) in red 977
pile, Rauma Rye yarn (750 m/kg) in various colors (see below)
Rauma Åkle yarn (1,750 m/kg) in various colors (see below)
Rauma prydvevgarn (3,000 m/kg) in various colors (see below)
Växbo Lin linen 12/2 (3,600 m/kg) in lime and unbleached
Växbo Lin linen 12/1 (7200 m/kg) in golden
Butterflies: Black: 1 strand Rye 516 + 2 strands Åkle 736
Green: 1 strand Rye 556 + 2 strands Åkle 783 + 1 strand 12/2 linen in lime
Red: 1 strand Rye 577 + 1 strand Åkle 739 + 2 strands prydvev 676
Yellow: 1 strand Rye 531 + 2 strands Åkle 746 + 1 strand 12/2 linen in lime
White: 2 strands Rye 501 + 1 strand prydvev 601 + 3 strands 12/1 linen in golden
Ombré A: 2 strands Rye 504 + 1 strand Åkle 703 + 2 strands 12/2 linen, unbl.
Ombré B: 1 strand Rye 504 + 2 strands Åkle 703 + 2 strands 12/2 linen, unbl.
Ombré C: 3 strands Åkle 703 + 3 strands 12/2 linen, unbleached
Ombré D: 1 strand Rye 501 + 2 strands Åkle 703 + 2 strands 12/2 linen, unbl.
Edge: 1 strand Åkle 746 + 1 strand 12/2 linen, unbleached

Reed : 8-dent (1 end per heddle, 1 end per dent), or 30/10, 1-1
Sett : 3 ends per ⅜ in / 1 cm (about 8 epi)
Ends : 164 to knot around + 4 edge + 4 selvedge (2 ends per
          heddle, 2 ends per dent x 1 on each selvedge) = 172
Width : About 22½ in / 57 cm
Knot Density : 15 knots per 4 in / 10 cm in both width and length
Threading : Straight draw

WEAVING: Tension the warp as much as you possibly can. All the tabby weft should be laid in arcs to avoid draw-in. "Weave" with 2-4 sticks
before you begin to even out the warp ends. Then weave 6-8 picks of
weft-faced rep with the same yarn as in the warp, 8/5 linen. Weave ¾ in
/ 2 cm weft-faced rep with one of your edge butterflies, and let it hang
down from the right side; it will build up the right selvedge. Change shed
and add the other edge butterfly on the left side; both butterflies should
run *under* the outermost selvedge in their neutral state.

WORKING PROCEDURE: First, you build up a "vessel" for the knot row
by weaving a few rows on the edges. The edge butterflies should only
run back and forth across the outermost 3 ends (the doubled selvedge
ends and 2 more). Four picks should be enough, but you can use 6 every
now and then if you think that the edges are too sparse.

    Now you're ready to tie knots! If you're using a ruler, hang it up
with a big loop made of the linen 8/5 threaded through the ruler. Hang
it over one of the brackets for the beater. If you tie knots back and forth
like I do, the loop has to be able to move from one side to the other. It's
best to start with the ruler far to one side, which makes it easier to wrap
the butterfly around it.

    I knot with the warp in a neutral position, without any treadles
lowered. The knot is made in the same way as with Miriam's rya (see
page 70), but if you use a ruler, the butterfly begins under it (on the side
nearest you), loops over to make the knot in the warp on the other side,
and then you pull the butterfly back under the ruler again and pull really,
really hard. Tie each knot around two warp ends and use all the ends,
i.e. don't hop over any in between. Try to learn how to knot to the right
in one row and to the left the next: it's better for your body and your
brain, and you'll save a little bit of yarn. If you're going to use the same
color for many rows, you don't have to cut off the butterfly; you just
start making knots again, right where you left off the row before.

    When a knot row is finished, beat as hard as you can with the
beater. Next is the tabby. I usually use a rug shuttle for the tabby weft,

often with single-wound rug wool. Rauma's *ullspiss* yarn is thinner than other brands' rug yarn, which is why I chose to wind this tabby weft double. Two tabby picks are enough between the knot rows, in this case. In both my flossa and rya patterns, I've used 3 warp ends on either side to build my edges on (see page 71), but I have the edge butterfly meet and interlock with the weft further in toward the center of the weaving so the edge will be extra strong. In order to avoid excess build up, which will make the weaving uneven, the edge yarn and the tabby weft first meet 3 knots from the edge on one side, then 2 knots from the edge on the other side, 1 knot on the next, 3 knots on the next, and so on.

Now you can slice those loops! I suggest you learn how to cut in both directions, although I can only cut in one. If you use a flossa knife, you simply put the blade between the strips of the ruler with the shield on the warp ends (not on the weaving and pull. Begin the process again with the vessel-building and tie your knots according to the working sketch. After the next-to-last row, cut off and bury the end of the tabby weft; you won't use it after the last knot row. After the last row, bury one of the edge butterflies and weave ⅜ in / 1 cm weft-faced rep across the whole width of the loom with the other. Finish with 6-8 picks of 8/5 linen. When you cut down, leave at least 7¾ in / 20 cm of warp to do your finishing with.

FINISHING: Remove all but 2 of the 8/5 picks so that the edge is straight and looks clean. Tie the warp ends together two by two with overhand knots. Follow the instructions for finishing rugs on page 74, which also work for linen warps.

Sketch with geometric shapes made in collage, which suits flossa's pix-elated feeling.

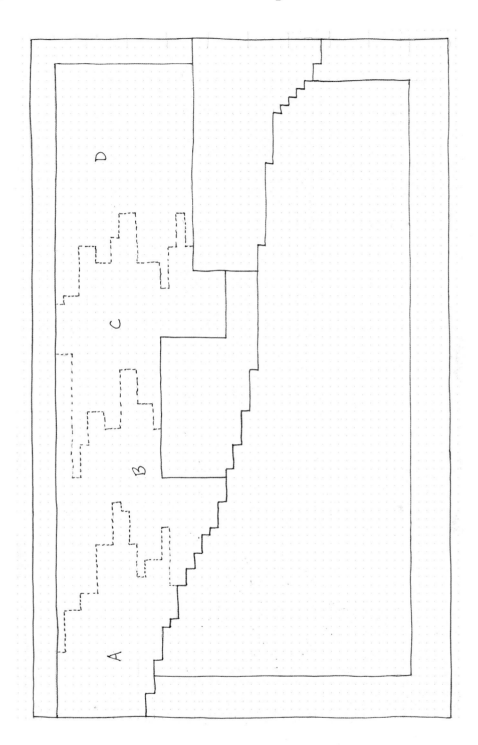

Making technical sketches for rugs is one of my favorite steps in the weaving process. Here I've translated the sketch's proportions to a certain number of squares. One square = one knot in this technical sketch. (Turn the book to make the sketch face the right way).

Rya Bath Mat

Linen is a very absorbent material and easy to wash, even in the machine. It's a fun challenge to put time and energy toward making things that we normally buy cheaply—in this case, a bath mat. Don't use your best scissors to cut the loops on this project, as they will quickly become dull from cutting so much linen.

Technique : Rya with a tabby base
Size in loom : 22½ × 34¼ in / 57 × 87 cm
Warp : Holma-Helsinglands linen warp 8/5 (950 m/kg)
Weft : Tabby, Borgs rug linen 4/6 (400 m/kg) in olive 1000
pile, Växbo Lin linen 12/2 (3,600 m/kg) in lime, unbleached, umber
Växbo Lin 12/1 (7,200 m/kg) in golden, umber
I also dyed unbleached 12/2 and golden 12/1 with Levafix, Scarlet-Brilliant Yellow CA 4:4 ratio in 0.5%, 0.3%, and 0.1% strengths
Butterflies: Lime: 6 strands lime 12/2 + 2 strands unbleached 12/2
Natural: 5 strands unbleached 12/2 + 6 strands golden 12/1
Umber: 5 strands umber 12/2 + 6 strands umber 12/1
Dyed, each strength: 5 strands 12/2 + 6 strands 12/1
Edge butterflies: 4 strands umber 12/2 + 2 strands unbleached 12/2 and 1 strand lime 12/2
Reed : 8-dent (1 end per heddle and 1 end per dent) or 30/10, 1-1
Sett : 3 ends per ⅜ in / 1 cm (about 8 epi)
Ends : 172, same as the flossa on page 86 (see note below)
Width in Reed : 22½ in / 57 cm
Knot Density : 10 knots per 4 in / 10 cm widthwise, 7 knots per 4 in / 10 cm lengthwise
Picks : About 4 picks per ⅜ in / 1 cm. The knot row + 5 tabby picks = ½ in / 1.5 cm
Threading : Straight draw

WEAVING : I wove this rya and the flossa project (page 86) with the same warp. Flossa is most often woven by knotting around pairs of warp ends without skipping any in between. Traditionally, rya is woven around pairs of warp ends with one warp end between (although this can vary, of course!), which is what I've done here, each row ending with a knot. Otherwise, you can follow the same working procedure. I don't usually use a ruler for knotting rya, but instead let the loops on the "active" row just cover the knot of the previous row. I leave the clipping of loops until the end and do it in one fell swoop.

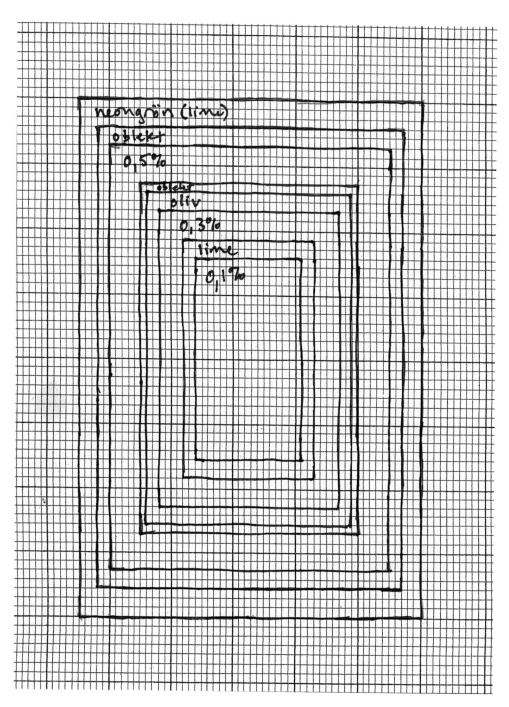

Another way to sketch rugs is to begin by making shapes on graph paper. Sometimes I don't even use any color, but instead see what yarns I have and work from there. This kind of paper is called "rya paper," and the squares have the "correct" measurements for the knot density I prefer, the same one I used in the bath mat project. The slightly rectangular squares allow for 1 square = 1 knot, and the sketch will actually look like the finished project.

Waffle Weave

I discovered waffle weave early in my time at Friends of Handicraft, and it quickly became a favorite technique. I've since made innumerable projects using the same tie-up, but with very different finished products depending on the material, the sett and pick count, the finishing, and so on. The opportunity for variation is as liberating as it is challenging.

Here are three projects that all use the same waffle weave draft. They require 5 shafts and 8 treadles. The tie-up, threading, and treadling is the same for all three. The differences are partly in number of ends and sett/pick count, but the choice of material is what really affects the usage and aesthetic of each piece. Linen waffle weave softens somewhat in the wash but retains its squared quality, while cotton shrinks and crinkles. But my wool waffle weave makes the longest visual journey, from airy and rectangular in the loom to dense and wavy after a tour of the washing machine.

I usually warp this version of waffle weave with 4 ends in my hand, since the threading is based on groups of 8 ends. If you've never warped with more than 2 ends at a time, try it! But it works with "only" 2 in your hand as well, of course.

Washcloth

The first project I ever wove in waffle weave was a washcloth. Linen is the perfect material to work with, and the color effect from the dyeing breaks up the repetitiveness of the structure. To prepare for dyeing, I made skeins of the yarn in different sizes, enough for the entire warp and part of the weft. I tied off the skeins with a lazy version of what the Japanese call *kasuri*, aiming for randomness of reserved areas. Then I dyed them with indigo.

Technique : Waffle weave

Size in loom : 14½ × 15 in / 37 × 38 cm

Warp : Växbo Lin linen 12/2 (3,600 m/kg) in unbleached, dyed with indigo

Weft : Växbo Lin linen 12/2 (3,600 m/kg) in unbleached, some dyed with indigo as in the warp

Reed : 12-dent (1 end per heddle, 2 ends per dent) or 45/10, 1-2 (can use 30/10, 1-3 but not in presleying)

Sett : 9 ends per ⅜ in / 1 cm (about 24 epi)

Ends : 336 + 1 to complete = 337

Width in Reed : 14½ in / 37 cm

Picks : 6 picks per ⅜ in / 1 cm in plain weave (about 15 ppi), 7 ends per ⅜ in / 1 cm in waffle (about 18 ppi)

Threading : Pointed twill, see the draft on page 130

Weaving : Weave 1½ in / 4 cm in plain weave, then 11¾ in / 30 cm in waffle weave according to the draft, and finish with 1½ in / 4 cm in plain weave. If you weave many in a row, place a contrasting pick between each for easier finishing.

Finishing : Zigzag on either side of each contrasting pick and raw edge. Cut into separate pieces and hem by hand. Can be washed in the machine on warm, with like colors if you've dyed with indigo. Line dry for more exfoliation, dry in the machine for a softer washcloth.

Bath Towel

Waffle weave is both beautiful and useful; the structure absorbs moisture well and it exfoliates gently. Here, I've made the waffle squares larger than in machine-woven waffle weave, which makes the towel fluffier and cozier. It draws in dramatically after washing, which I've accounted for in the measurements here.

Technique : Waffle weave

Size in loom : 37½ × 67 in / 95 × 170 cm

Warp : Ekelunds organic cotton 8/2 (6,400 m/kg) in ecru 1218

Weft : Ekelunds organic cotton 8/2 (6,400 m/kg) in mint green 6114

Reed : 12-dent (1 end per heddle, 2 ends per dent) or 50/10, 1-2

Sett : 10 ends per ⅜ in / 1 cm (about 24 epi)

Ends : 952 in pattern + 1 to complete = 953

Width in Reed : 37½ in / 95 cm

Picks : 8 picks per ⅜ in / 1 cm (about 15 epi) in both plain weave and waffle

Threading : Pointed twill, see page 130

Weaving : Weave 4 in / 10 cm in plain weave, then 59 in / 150 cm in waffle weave according to the draft, and finish with 4 in / 10 cm in plain weave. If you weave more than one, place a contrasting pick in between for easier finishing.

Finishing : Zigzag on either side of the contrasting picks and raw edges. Don't forget a loop for hanging, if you'd like it; I prefer to sew those on with the machine. Hem by hand. Wash in the machine on warm. Let hang dry instead of in the machine so that it doesn't shrink to the size of a hand towel.

Shawl

This project is a challenge for your command of the shuttle and a good exercise in beating loosely. The shawl is woven very loosely to create the perfect conditions for machine felting. The felting gives the shawl a very cool look, but also makes it like a warm embrace. The shawl shrinks a lot in the machine—around 35% in length and 50% in width. Remember to leave a little warp on the end when you cut down if you want fringe. I suggest you weave two small samples at the beginning and then wash one but not the other, as a reference for future projects. Not all wool singles felt the same way either, so try a few different ones.

Technique : Waffle weave
Size in loom : 35½ × 137 in (3.8 yds) / 90 × 350 cm (3.5 m)
Warp : Borgs Mora worsted 20/2 (9,000 m/kg) in pink 2015
Weft : Ekenäs Hantverk Gotland wool singles (4,200 m/kg)
Reed : 9-dent (1 end per heddle, 2 ends per dent) or 35/10, 1-2
Sett : 7 ends per ⅜ in / 1 cm (about 18 epi)
Ends : 632 + 1 to complete = 633
Width in Reed : 35½ in / 90 cm
Picks : 5 picks per ⅜ in / 1 cm (about 13 ppi)
Threading : Pointed twill, see the draft on page 130
Weaving : Begin by weaving a sample—for example, 1¼ in / 3 cm plain weave, 2½ in / 6 cm waffle, 1¼ in / 3 cm plain weave. If you want fringe, "weave" a few sticks in between the sample and the "real" weaving. Otherwise, you can just use a contrasting pick. Then weave according to the following table:

PLAIN WEAVE	WAFFLE
4 IN / 10 CM	
	23½ IN / 60 CM
11¾ IN / 30 CM	
	23½ IN / 60 CM
11¾ IN / 30 CM	
	23½ IN / 60 CM
11¾ IN / 30 CM	
	23½ IN / 60 CM
4 IN / 10 CM	

<u>Finishing</u> : When you cut down, leave as much warp at the end as you did at the beginning for fringe, if desired. Zigzag the raw edges (even if you have fringe) with gray thread that matches the weft; the thread will hide in the felted fabric later. I left the fringe as it was without braiding or twisting, and it also felted together in a weird and beautiful way. If you want braided fringe, braid before washing.

Now you're going to break all the rules about wool and washing machines! Throw the shawl in the machine with a little well-worn hand towel and the sample, if you made one—but nothing more. Use a bit of detergent (it doesn't have to be wool detergent) and wash on warm (104 degrees F / 40 degrees C). Pull lightly at the edges if you think it's shrunk a little too much, and dry as flat as possible.

Double Weave Shawl

Double weave is a technique that can seem hard to wrap your head around before you've woven it—and okay, even afterward! This version is called "squared double weave" (*rutig dubbelväv*) in Swedish, which means that part of the two different layers change places with each other when you treadle the different blocks, forming squares. You can clearly see the two different layers in the finished fabric. I've chosen to use the same weft in both blocks so that you only have one shuttle to keep track of, but also to achieve the "disappearing" color effect. This variation requires 8 shafts and treadles.

Technique : Squared double weave ("checkerboard windows" in English)

Size in loom : 26 × 59 in / 66 × 150 cm

Warp : Borgs Mora worsted 20/2 (9,500 m/kg) in white, some dyed with Färgkraft dyes, Ochre—Marine Blue 1:7, 0.1% strength, dip-dyed (see note below). Calculate for 80% of the yarn weight (instead of 100%) because you won't dye the entire warp chain.

Weft : Borgs Mora worsted 20/2 (9,500 m/kg) in white

Reed : 12-dent (1 end per heddle, 4 ends per dent) or 50/10, 1-4

Sett : 20 ends per ⅜ in / 1 cm total, 10 ends per ⅜ in / 1 cm per layer (48 epi total, 24 epi each layer)

Ends : 1320 total, 660 in each layer

Width in Reed : 26 in / 66 cm

Picks : 16 picks per ⅜ in / 1 cm total, 8 picks per ⅜ in / 1 cm in each layer (about 40 ppi total, 20 ppi per layer)

Threading : See the draft on page 131

Warp each layer separately. They should be the same color, but one of the layers will be dip-dyed. I usually separate my warp chains across the breadth of the warp, but in this case it's more important to get an even color in one whole layer, so I warped all 660 ends to dye them. The undyed layer should also be warped as one chain and should be tied off as described in the beginning of the book.

The chain that will be dyed should be tied and prepared in a special way. For my loom and this project, each of my warp chains was 98 in (2.75 yd) / 250 cm (2.5 m) long, but your loom may be different. The traditional tight tie-offs are necessary to avoid the chain tangling in the bath, but they will make a white line if they end up in the section that will be dyed. The ties around the cross and at the end of the warp won't affect the weaving, but your mid-warp ties should be about 20 in / 50 cm from the end with the cross, and 3 in / 8 cm from the other end, with none in the middle. Those tie-offs end up in the loom waste. I dyed almost the entire chain, up to about 15¾ in / 40 cm from the tie-off near the cross. I dye the non-cross end of that warp chain so it's easier to thread the two different layers later.

PRE-SLEYING AND BEAMING DOUBLE WEAVE WITHOUT TWO YARN BEAMS: If you're going to weave a lot of double weave, it's beneficial to have two yarn beams, but I only have one. In this project, I pre-sleyed one full chain and then the other in the same 12-dent or 50/10 reed. That is, I pre-sleyed the white chain first with 4 ends (in their loop) in every other dent, and this chain got its own pair of leasing sticks. Then I pre-sleyed the dyed chain in the empty dents between the white ends in the same reed, and this chain also got its own pair of leasing sticks. When you put the warp in the loom, each chain needs its own back stick. When you thread, you take every other thread from each chain. Follow the threading draft on page 131.

WEAVING: Follow the chart below. Block A is on Treadles 5-8, and Block B is on Treadles 1-4.

BLOCK A	BLOCK B
3.5 IN / 9 CM (HEM)	
	2¼ IN / 5.5 CM (44 PICKS/LAYER)
¼ IN / 0.75 CM (6 PICKS/LAYER)	
	2¼ IN / 5.5 CM
3.5 IN / 9 CM (HEM)	

REPEATED FOR A TOTAL OF 49½ IN / 125 CM

FINISHING: When you weave Block A, the fabric becomes like a tube, so when you hem this piece you separate the layers and zigzag around the entire tube. Then fold in about ¼ in / 0.5 cm and sew together the two layers with a whipstitch.

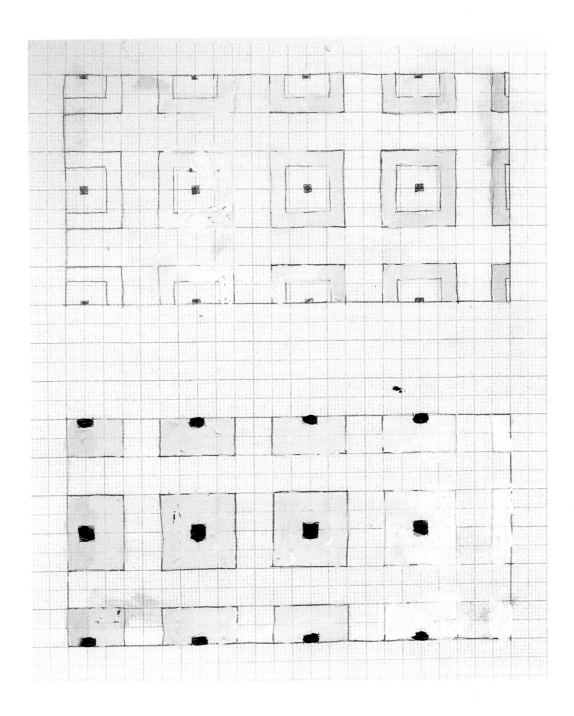

Sometimes I begin with a simple shape I like, drawn on graph paper. Then
I photocopy the sketch and paint it in different ways. This is a sketch
for a rug that I ended up using as inspiration for a squared double weave
shawl similar to the one on page 104.

Design Process

MIRIAM: In the book *Trasmattor och andra mattor* [Rag rugs and other rugs], from 1958, the author writes: "It is a waste of money to put material and time toward unartistic patterns and poor fabric quality. Therefore, we offer you here patterns drawn by the well-respected artist Ingrid Dessau." I love buying old weaving books at flea markets, looking at the funky colors in the analogue photographs and being enchanted by names like "Cuba," "Harlequin," and "Samba." But, luckily, opinions about who is allowed to design and make textiles have changed quite a bit since then.

We want to do more than just offer new thoughts and ideas about weaving—we also want to present those thoughts and ideas in a different way. In this chapter I go over the elements and techniques I use to design textiles, and how you can dig even deeper and use what I call a "creative cycle."

FOUNDATION: A LIBRARY OF FORM AND COLOR

For me, weaving offers painting-like possibilities: the warp is the paper, and the weft is the paint. Nothing except the simple, clean tabby structure needs to be decided beforehand, when you let your hand steer and your head follow. When I am asked about what inspires me, I usually answer that it is the aesthetic of the 1940s-60s, nature, and whatever is happening around me. A longer, but better and more detailed answer could be, "The movement of the yellow-green seagrass that sways against the cliffs where I lie, partially cold, partially warm, at the seaside in the summer on the High Coast." Or "My friend's outfit, suddenly matching a brightly sunlit wall, the colors blending into the same color spectrum, while at the same time the corner of a roof forms a sharp, angled shadow headed the same direction as my friend's shirt collar." Similarly, "orange and turquoise" is the short answer to the question of what my favorite colors are. The real answer is, "the shade created when two colors overlap"—any colors, that is, since the matte, gritty and endlessly deep, or completely light shade created when two colors are layered contain everything I dream about in terms of color. Colors find their way to different memories and feelings, and are spun together with desire in my brain, into a thread that is transported to my hand.

Ebba von Eckermann, "The Weaving Countess" whose handwoven skirts and blankets were extremely popular during the 1950s and 1960s, said that she "wove mostly during the winter, when [she] was hungriest for color." Color is fundamental, so much more than something you just choose randomly. Color is mighty and infinite.

To be able to preserve and be reminded of these elements in my studio, I have books about different people and places sitting within easy reach of my loom, along with magazine clippings and postcards on the wall, stones and shells on my desk, and small woven samples that either belong with the photos or happened to be a good combination. It can get to be quite busy, but it helps. Whenever I find myself just standing at my loom, shuttle in hand, staring into space, I can turn around and see the composition of sketches and feelings that inspire what I'm weaving, or thumb through one of my go-to books and feel how the call to action returns. Similarly, I like to have a range of coffee cups so that I can choose the color and shape that feels best any given day; I often realize afterward that I've chosen a cup that matches both what I'm wearing and what I'm weaving. By thinking of color and shape as constantly present, you make them consistently available to you.

REFERENCE LIBRARY

Books have the same tactile value as textiles. Having books on hand is like having a friend in creativity, and in addition to advice and practical help, they can also fulfill a psychological function. My four favorites from my bookshelf are books about Veronica Nygren, Tove Jansson, Mary Blair, and Georgia O'Keeffe. In their pages, I can find sketches and commentary, snapshots of daily life and sunsets, evidence of self-doubt and luck, processes, and results. These four women have in common a tremendous eye for color and magnificent works of art. But what helps me most when I flip through these books is the reminder of the point of creating: that a little sketch can be as important as the finished piece, and that being true to yourself is always, always worthwhile.

PHOTOS AND DIGITAL ARCHIVE

I use my phone daily to save and document my inspiration. I take photos of colors, shapes, angles, surfaces, structures, feelings, encounters, and occurrences—simple snapshots that I either edit in an app or just save in the camera roll. I may organize them in a special album, or I may forget about them, only to find them a year later and get inspired again.

I use Stories on Instagram the same way. It's an easy format in which to share photos and videos, where you can also add text, colors, and animated GIFs. They are only available for 24 hours, but they are saved in their own archive in the app, which I often look at. The things I document in Stories are often of a more spontaneous and compassionate character than the posts I put up in my main feed, and they function as a catalyzer for things I've forgotten six months later.

Instagram also has a "Save" function that allows you to book-mark and save other users' photos to your own archive, which is a perfect way to collect inspiration. But don't worry that this may be stealing or copying; it's just a digital way to rip a picture out of a magazine and paste it into your sketchbook. On top of all of that, Instagram is a very luxurious way to make connections and find like-minded folks. I have friends on Instagram that I've never met in real life, but whom I can bounce ideas off of.

Pinterest is another straightforward and easily manageable source for collecting pictures. Once you've installed the app on your phone, you always have rich material at hand, both the things you've saved into different folders and the search results you can turn up from among its millions of pictures. I have folders with names like, "Posters, Colors, Fonts," where I collect graphic design and art, "Inspiration for School," where I've collected everything weaving-re-lated since I was in school, and "Pools," which consists entirely of various dreamy pictures of different kinds of outdoor pools.

TO SKETCH

A sketch can be painted, drawn in pencil, drawn in pastel, photo-graphed, drawn in pen, woven, folded, and glued. It can be a picture composed for and drawn directly in the rectangular shape of a rug, or a zoomed-in photograph of the corner of a doodle on scratch paper. It can also be a real little weaving, a sample made in a frame loom or on threads wound around a piece of cardboard. Arianna likes to make collages when she has time to and when she chooses to sketch in color; otherwise, a few lines in pencil or pen on squared graph paper is enough to help her keep track of the shapes she wants to work with. I might make multiple pages' worth of collage and sketches in my sketchbook, or on loose-leaf paper, before I decide what I want to do for a specific project. My favorite media for sketching for textiles are:

TOMBOW PENS: These are liquid ink pens with two felt tips, one soft, long, and brush-like and the other thin and hard. The color is

transparent, and the colors don't mix when you apply them in layers. That is, blue and red don't become purple, but rather new shades of blue and red. Of all the pens I've tried, I think these are the absolute best. I always have a little bundle of them with me that I use when I take notes at meetings and when I write lists; that kind of spontaneous use often leads to color combinations I later use in sketches.

PASTELS Perfect for sketching rya, rölakan, and other kinds of weaving in wool. The energetic structure of the pastel strokes, which can't be completely controlled, reminds me of long tufts of yarn in unconstrained rya-motion. If you choose water-soluble pastels, you can paint over them with a wet brush to combine colors, creating more fluid sections of your sketches, and then after it's dried, go back over the sketch with a dry pastel. You can see an example of this on page 9.

COLORED PENCILS: On vacation and trips, I like to bring along good-quality colored pencils—they must have high pigment content. It takes a little more work to achieve real depth and surfaces with them, something I don't normally have the time or the patience for. Colored pencils also have a lovely textile feeling, and can also be used in layers, as long as you start with a light touch and gradually press harder.

WOVEN SKETCHES: Sometimes when I'm working on a large, time-consuming weaving and start to feel fed up, or when I suddenly get an idea I have to test out right away, I make a little woven sketch. I make a simple warp and a miniature weaving, partially for a change of pace from the large weaving I'm working on, partially to quickly gain an understanding of how a certain yarn looks as rya pile. You can wrap strands of yarn around a piece of cardboard or a sponge, or around two pens that have been taped to the table, as in the photo on the next page. To make a shed, you can use more pens, empty bobbins, or something similar. Then you can start weaving! Pick up warp threads with your fingers or use a needle. You can even make these kinds of samples when you're on the go.

SKETCH BOOKS: Keeping a continuous sketchbook where you sketch, plan weaving drafts, and write down words and thoughts is not only the perfect way to keep everything orderly and in the same place, but is also a method of assessing your process as a whole. Don't get stuck on making every page perfect and tidy; that will only make it hard to get started. Just fill it up! I have a Leuchtturm sketchbook of A5 paper in my studio, and one of A6 paper in my bag. In the big one, I

mostly sketch, and in the little one, I write meeting notes, jot down reminders, and make various sitting-on-the-train sketches. Often, it's the little one that follows along when I'm on vacation. And when even the boring information is written down with nice pens, the sketchbook, with its lists of stuff to buy and beach scenes from a vacation in Crete in September 2018, is a little artwork in and of itself. Cyclical!

FROM SKETCH TO WEAVING: IN PRACTICE

To translate a sketch to a weaving, I mainly use one of two methods: gridded or freehand. Gridded is good for rya. I calculate how long and how wide I want the rya to be, and multiply that by the number of ends per centimeter in the warp. That tells me how many knots will be in each row, and how many rows will fill the length. I can then make a grid using that information in Illustrator or Photoshop. I photograph or scan the sketch if it's not already digital, and then over that I lay a grid that is, for example, 45 rows high and 76 rows wide. Each square represents one knot, and that makes it easy to see exactly what colors that square/knot contains. If you are after as close a translation as possible from sketch to weaving, it's very important to consider the number of knots. Keep in mind that rya is like a perler bead board or pixels: the more squares/knots, the higher the "resolution." So if it looks like there are quite a few different colors or shades in the same square, you probably need to increase the number of squares (and thus knots). However, textile translations of a sketch can be interpreted in many ways, so don't get stuck on the sketch being exact and perfect.

I usually have both the gridded sketch and the original sketch in front of me at the loom so I don't "forget" how the sketch looks without all those squares on top. Begin with the bottom row, making knot after knot along the row. When you're done, cross out that row and go up to the next one. If I have a ton of squares and a complicated pattern, I usually keep my place with a pin, not least to keep track of where I stopped weaving the day before.

You can also make a gridded sketch by hand. The sketch can be directly drawn onto graph paper, or you can outline the different sections on tracing paper and tape it to a piece of graph paper. With this method, you do have to take the dimensions and scale of the design into consideration from the beginning. The elements of the sketch in both breadth and width are multiplied by the dimensions that you want the woven piece to have. To calculate the scale: if the sketch is around 6¼ in / 16 cm wide and the finished piece will be around 31¼ / 80 cm wide, you can divide 31¼ by 6¼ (or 80 by 16) and get 5. The scale of the sketch is therefore 1:5, which means every inch / cm of the sketch represents 5 inches / cm in the weaving. Normally, graph paper squares are ¼ in / 0.5 cm tall and ¼ in / 0.5 cm wide. The length of four of those squares, 1 inch in the sketch (or two squares, 1 cm in the sketch), translates to 5 inches (or 5 cm) in the weaving. This works well for geometric shapes and sketches with distinct borders and central motifs. It's easy to think of as "four squares of blue, then two squares of brown, and then four squares of blue again." For more abstract or fluid forms, you'll need "higher resolution," or more squares/knots. There is graph paper with even smaller squares that's better for that kind of design.

The other method, freehand, is exactly as the name suggests: free. For the tapestry "Teotitlán/Rocío y los colores fuertes" that can be seen in the background of our author photo on page 6, I began with a painting as my sketch, but quickly gave that up because it felt too restrictive and closed off. The picture I wanted to weave came from the experience I had had riding a bus from Oaxaca to the village of Teotitlán del Valle, where I had an internship working with weavers: a bumpy ride through yellow-brown fields, flickering agave plantations, and meter-high cacti, with bright sun and the blue mountains in the distance. Following a sketch and making diagonal lines with the loom's beater just wouldn't work. I began to use a pick-up method and built up each shape separately. I used wool rug yarn and mixed many different colors in each butterfly, which filled the warp more than it could handle, so it began to bulge. The result was an undulating weaving that was just as crazy, alive, warm, challenging, and fantastic as that experience on the bus.

For the *slitrya* blanket on page 81, I used the watercolor sketch on page 83, which has a relatively clear division: about one third lake, one third mountains, one third sky. The dimensions of the weaving were already decided, so I figured it would work to just split the length of the weaving up into thirds and weave freely. I had planned for the finished piece to be 51¼ in / 130 cm long, but when I was done with the lake, it was already 35½ in / 90 cm long! That was not exactly a third of my expected total. Luckily, I always use a longer warp than I need. The finished piece was more than 2 yards / 2 meters long, but so much better than if the weaving had been its planned length. A freehand translation almost always results in something unforeseen, with a quality that can't be planned or forced.

SKETCHING METHOD: *SLITRYA*

METHOD 1. NATURE: Choose a photo or a memory of a place. Decide the ambiance: is it summer, fall, spring, or winter? Warm or cool light? Morning, afternoon, or evening? Is this is Sweden or somewhere else? Is it a real place or somewhere in a dream? Use this to develop a color scale. Next, make a sketch of the picture in your head using the medium you prefer. Add a grid or keep the sketch as it is if you'd rather work freehand.

METHOD 2. DIGITAL PRODUCTION: Work from a photo. Test out manipulating it in different ways. Zoom in, take a screenshot, and save it. Zoom in again and take a new screenshot. Edit the contrast, light, shadows, warmth, and atmosphere in an app. Put it into a collage and tile the image so that it repeats. Make a mirror image and turn it upside down. By testing and playing in this way, the image becomes more than just a "pretty picture," and the colors, shapes, and compositions that weren't apparent at first begin to show themselves. Add a grid or keep the sketch as it is if you'd rather work freehand.

For the rya cushion on page 72, I was inspired by the public art in the town square in Årsta, as well as the colors in a fashion photograph from the 1950s. With my Tombow pens, I pulled out the colors I wanted and sketched a few geometric and abstract versions, but none of them felt quite right. Instead I chose to weave and knot freely. But in retrospect, it's clear that the preparatory work—the sketches—ended up as the foundation for how it turned out.

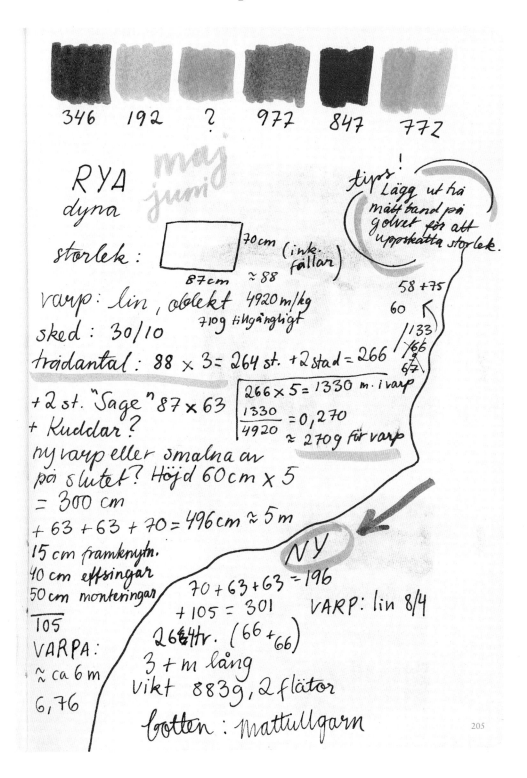

346   192   ?   977   847   772

RYA
dyna

maj juni

tips!
Lägg ut ha
mått band på
golvet för att
uppskatta storlek.

storlek :
  70cm (inkl. fällar)
87cm ≈ 88

58 + 75
60

varp: lin, oblekt 4920 m/kg
710g tillgängligt

sked : 30/10
trådantal : 88 × 3 = 264 st. + 2 stad = 266

133
66
67

$266 × 5 = 1330$ m. i varp
$\dfrac{1330}{4920} = 0,270$
≈ 270g för varp

+ 2 st. "Sage" 87 × 63
+ Kuddar ?
ny varp eller smalna av
på slutet? Höjd 60cm × 5
= 300 cm
+ 63 + 63 + 70 = 496cm ≈ 5m

15 cm framknytn.
40 cm efsingar
50 cm monteringar

105
VARPA:
≈ ca 6m
6,76

NY

70 + 63 + 63 = 196
+ 105 = 301
26 £4tr. ($66 + 66$)
3 + m lång
Vikt 883g, 2 flätor
botten : mattullgarn

VARP: lin 8/4

205

The draft is also part of the sketching work!

Dyeing

MIRIAM: Being able to dye your own yarn is a real asset in your weaving practice. You can create your own color scales, make magic with second-hand yarn of the wrong color, and add effects that make a big difference.

I learned how to dye at Friends of Handicraft School according to their well-documented process, which uses exact measurements of 1% solutions and 2% solutions mixed with 0.05% solutions in ratios of 1:7 and 7:1. Every step in the process is done in a precise order, and every chemical added at the chime of a timer. When I flip through my notes from those lessons, I am astounded by what a math whiz I apparently was back then—page after page of equations and ratios. It wasn't a bad introduction, and I ended up with a rich library of hues to use as a starting point. But in the meantime, I've developed my own method, which is not only less complicated but also better adapted to how I see and use color in my weaving. However, it should be said that my method is most suitable for dyeing for one specific work at a time, and with less than one kilo of yarn of each intended color. Dyeing many kilos of yarn of the same color at once is best done according to instructions from the production company for your dye; my dyes come from Färgkraft, and instructions for their dyes can be found on their website.

I never use dye recipes or scales. Instead, I begin by selecting the color categories and spectrums that are in the sketch or idea I'm basing my piece on. The color categories become the main dye baths that I use as a foundation. Instead of calculating exact percentages, I use two different methods to achieve different hues of each color:

1. The different undertones of the yarns that are going to be dyed.
2. The natural gradation that occurs in the dyepot, from a dark and saturated first bath to a light and unsaturated last bath.

Dyeing different shades of white yarn, from chalk white to off-white and cream, in the same color results in a very authentic variation of hues. The different yellow tones inherent in the yarn affect the final color and contribute to the well-roundedness of the piece. Another example is deep greens, reds, and blues, which are best dyed on naturally brown yarn—in that case, you don't need as much pigment, since dark saturation is already present in the yarn.

If you make use of a dyebath from its darkest and most saturated to when there is barely any pigment left, you end up with a natural scale of the same shade from dark to light. For example, if you'd like a range from dark orange to very light coral pink, you begin by mixing up a saturated orange dye bath (by saturated, I mean that the bath is completely opaque). The yarn that will be dyed that darkest shade should be placed in the dye bath first and can pick up the excess pigment.

Depending on how many different gradations you want in your scale, after a little while you can add another skein in, with the first skein still in there to continue to pick up color. When you decide they are done and remove them to be rinsed and dried, you're left with a light dye bath that should be transparent but still retains some color. That means it's time to add the yarn that will be a light shade. When the dye bath is completely clear, all the pigment has been used up. This way, you don't waste dye, either.

At the outset, it may seem as though I'm wasting pigment because I don't weigh out the exact amount that I need, but the opposite is true. Everything is used. Even if I don't need light colors for a specific project, I dye them anyway—they'll surely be useful in another project (not to mention all the color combinations that have emerged and planted the seeds for new projects because of this method of dyeing). Of course, this requires that you always have more yarn than you need for your current project, but if you're weaving with techniques like rya, extra yarn is always needed.

1.   On the table: large pots, chemical pigments for wool and silk from Färgkraft AB (in Sweden), jars to mix colors in, spoons and other tools for stirring, rubber gloves, the yarn you'll be dyeing, and some scrap yarn of the same quality to test the colors on. The yarns that I'll be dyeing with in these photos are: one skein of chalk-white plied wool rug yarn, one skein of off-white single-ply wool rug yarn, a small skein of rusty-orange wool rug yarn, and a small skein of light brown 5-ply wool yarn. The pigments that I'm using are brown, blue-green, and ochre.

2.   Tie off the skeins in 3-4 places so they don't tangle. If you don't want a reserve-dyeing effect, tie lightly so the yarn still can move around but won't tangle. Put all the skeins in a warm bath with a few drops of wool washing liquid (with a PH below 7) to neutralize the yarn before it will be dyed with this pigment, which is acidic. If you're dyeing wool, it needs to be washed first to remove any excess grease. Wool is naturally greasy, to protect sheep from damp and keep them warm; however, this can also prevent pigment from penetrating the yarn.

3.   Mix your colors, just like you would if you were using watercolors. Keep in mind that pigments are a bit like spices in food—a little goes a long way. Start with a very small amount and increase gradually. Add a bit of water and stir to dissolve the pigment. Some are harder

to dissolve and need to be worked with a spoon or a little spatula. How does the color look? Is it correct? If not, add a bit more pigment. I mixed two colors, a turquoise-petrol out of blue-green and a little ochre, and a saffron orange with ochre and brown pigment.

4. Fill two pots halfway with water and put them on the burners. Set the burners to medium. Add the dye mixture and then the appropriate chemicals. Traditionally, these are sodium sulfate (Glauber's salt), vinegar, and baylan for these specific pigments. The salt increases the yarn's ability to absorb the dye, the vinegar controls the acidity of the bath, and the baylan makes it such that the dye is absorbed at 176 degrees F / 80 degrees C instead of 194-212 degrees F / 90-100 degrees C, which is gentler on the yarn. I never use baylan, and I think the dye adheres anyway, even if the temperature isn't as hot; I haven't noted an issue with colorfastness thus far. I would use baylan when dyeing silk, however, since silk is much more sensitive to high temperatures. Instead of sodium sulfate, I use sodium chloride, i.e. table salt. If I don't have any vinegar, I use lemon or lime juice, like they do in Mexico.

5. When the bath is lukewarm, add the yarn. I put the off-white and the rust-orange skeins in the petrol-blue bath, and the white plied and light brown skeins in the saffron orange bath. Both dye mixtures are pretty light, not very saturated. The pots are relatively small, and I've chosen not to lift up and rotate the skeins because I want an uneven, variegated effect.

6. Maintain a high temperature, but not boiling, for about 10-30 minutes. When the water in the dye bath is clear, the dyeing is done.

7. Rinse the yarn under the tap and hang dry. With this method, you can dye an entire spectrum of color. This helps create maximized effects in your weaving; for example, you can shadow a light orange section with its own color, i.e., a dark orange in the same hue ("tint, tone, and shade").

"But how can you know that it's exactly the right color when you pull it out?" You *don't* know. But that's exactly the point. Dyeing is just one part of the anatomy and structure of weaving. You'll also need to take into account the blending of colors in a butterfly, the number of picks per inch / cm, how a color looks as a skein and how it looks as 1½ in

/ 4 cm-long pile placed here and there over a foot and a half / half a meter of rya—how it looks close up, and from many meters away. To be able to calculate this stuff in numbers beforehand is impossible: you have to see the color, not compute it.

ARIANNA: When I dye yarn, I use Levafix from Zenit for cellulose material like cotton and linen, and dye from Färgkraft for animal fibers like wool and silk. When I choose colors, I begin with a library of dyed yarns that I've built up over the years—but even when you follow a recipe to the letter, there are so many aspects that affect the color you end up with.

Cellulose fibers should be dyed at a low temperature for a long time, and in different steps. Animal fibers can be dyed for as little as 40 minutes, and all the pigment and chemicals can be thrown in at the beginning instead of in doses.

OTHER DYE EFFECTS

■ VARIEGATED YARN/CROWDED DYEING: Dyeing in a small pot and/or using a small amount of water intentionally will make the yarn unevenly dyed: mottled, variegated, marbled. This yarn gives your weaving a lively effect and is a very simplified version of reserve dyeing.

■ RESERVE DYEING: By knotting and covering ("reserving") parts of the yarn before dyeing, you can preserve the yarn's original color in those areas. A pattern, either spontaneous or planned, will emerge in your weaving while using these yarns. In its most advanced form, this is called *ikat* or *kasuri*, where extremely meticulous, extremely hard knots are tied in warp and/or weft and form intricate patterns in a range of colors, even though the piece may be woven in the most basic technique.

A simple form of reserve dyeing is to knot a skein hard in four places to get even white dots in your weaving, or to only dye one end of a skein for a striped effect.

Drafts

MIRIAM'S PLACEMATS, PAGE 50:

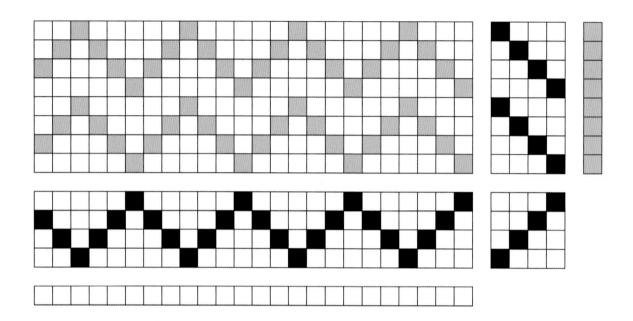

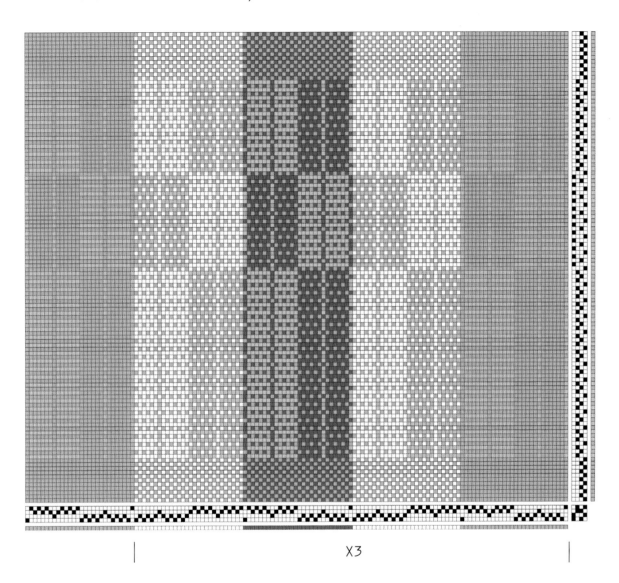

X3

In tie-up, Treadle 3 is Block A and Treadle 4 is Block B.

WAFFLE WEAVE:

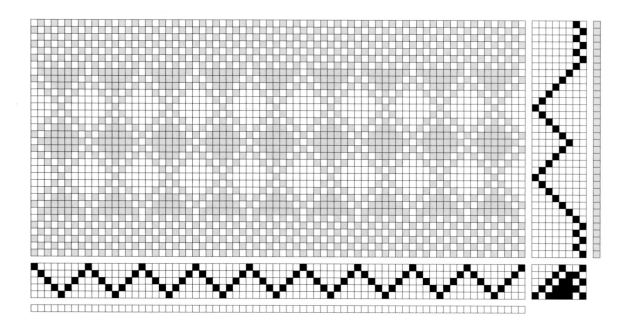

BINDING: Waffle weave on 5 shafts and 8 treadles.
Note: Start and end the waffle lots on Treadle 3.

DOUBLE WEAVE SHAWL, PAGE 105:

X29

PLAIN WEAVE:

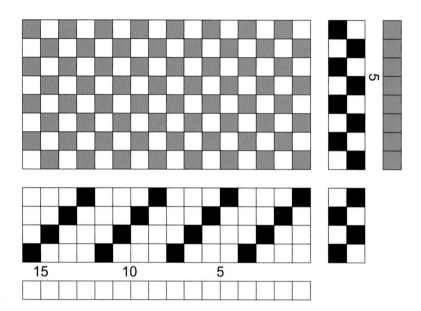

15   10   5

SHUTTLE-WOVEN PILLOW, PAGE 65:

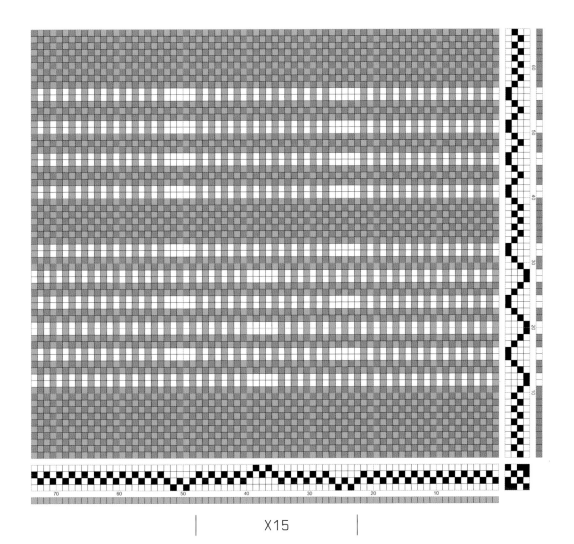

X15

Oaxaca placemats and napkins; see page 50.

Yarn Information & Bibliography

YARN

The yarns and fibers we used in this book came from:

Båvens Spinnhus
www.bavensspinnhus.se

Ekelunds Linneväveriet i Hörred
www.ekelunds.se

Ekenäs hantverk
www.ekenashantverk.se

Holma-Helsingland, Bockens Garner
www.holma.se

Rauma Ullvarefabrikk
www.raumagarn.no

Ullförmedlingen
www.ullformedlingen.se

Växbo Lin (ships internationally)
www.vaxbolin.se

Wålstedts Ullspinneri
www.walstedts.com

Östergötlands Ullspinneri (ships internationally)
www.ullspinneriet.se

Yarn distributors and other resources in the US and North America:

Lone Star Loom Room (Holma-Helsinglands)
www.lonestarloomroom.com

The Yarn Guys (Rauma)
www.theyarnguys.com

The Woolly Thistle (Rauma)
www.thewoollythistle.com

Vävstuga Weaving School
www.vavstuga.com

Some yarns and fibers—including Båvens, Ekelunds, Ekenäs hantverk, Ullförmedlingen, and Wålstedts—may be difficult to find. A variety of additional and substitute yarns are available from:
Webs—America's Yarn Store
75 Service Center Road
Northampton, MA 01060
800-367-9327
yarn.com

LoveKnitting.com
loveknitting.com/us

If you are unable to obtain any of the yarn or fiber used in this book, it can be replaced with another of a similar weight and composition. Please note, however, the finished projects may vary slightly from those shown, depending on the yarn or fiber used. Try www.yarnsub.com for suggestions.

For more information on selecting or substituting yarn or fiber, contact your local yarn shop or an online store; they are familiar with all types of yarns and fibers and would be happy to help you. Additionally, the online knitting community at Ravelry.com has forums where you can post questions about specific yarns and fibers. Yarns come and go so quickly these days and there are so many beautiful yarns available.

BIBLIOGRAPHY

Georgia O'Keeffe and Her Houses – Ghost Ranch and Abiquiui by Barbara Buhler Lynes and Agapita Lopez (Abrams and Georgia O'Keeffe Museum, 2012)

Magic, Color, Flair: the World of Mary Blair by John Canemaker (Disney editions, 2014)

Handbok i vävning, Bindningslära – konstvävnader by Ulla Cyrus-Zetterström (Natur & Kultur, 1990)

Våra vävda mattor, nordisk mattdesign by Pia Eldin and Anita Lundberg (ICA, 1991)

Warp and Weft: Lessons in Drafting for Handweaving by Mariana Eriksson, Gunnel Gustavsson, and Kerstin Lovallius (Trafalgar Square Books, 2011)

Väv gamla och glömda tekniker by Mariana Eriksson, Ulla Getzmann, Gunnel Gustavsson, and Kerstin Lovallius (Natur & Kultur, 1993)

Textila kuber och blixtar: rölakanets konst- och kulturhistoria by Viveka Hansen (Institutet för kulturforskning, 1992)

Veronica Nygren – Textil konst och radikal design by Hedvig Hedqvist et al (Atlantis, 2015)

Muminvärlden och verkligheten – Tove Jansons liv i bilder by Petter Karlsson (Max Ström, 2014)

Linnevävar by Ylva Kongbäck (Ica Bokförlag, 1998)

Den glömda kjolen – Ebba von Eckermann textilier 1950–1980 by Lotta Lewenhaupt (Signum, 2011)

Vi väver till hemmet by Maja Lundbäck (Ica Bokförlag, 1956)

Stora Vävboken by Laila Lundell and Elisabeth Windesjö (Ica Bokförlag, 2005)

Nock, Ragg, Rya – det glänser om ullen by Anttott Parholt and Eva Anderson (Föreningen Sveriges Hemslöjdskonsulenter UllMa, 2002)

Handvävt: vävmönster by Malin Selander (Wezäta, 1958)

A SELECTED GLOSSARY

BEAMING ON: When the warp is drawn or "beamed" onto the loom's yarn beam.

BOBBIN WINDER: Used to wind the weft onto bobbins, which are placed into a shuttle.

COUNTERMARCH: A type of weaving loom that controls how the shed is formed, lifting and sinking different shafts and warp ends. A countermarch both lifts and sinks warp ends, as opposed to a counterbalance, which only lowers warp ends to create different sheds.

CROSS: When warping, the threads form a fig-ure-eight at one end; this is called the cross. It keeps the warp ends in order. When the warp is in the loom, the cross is preserved and controlled by leasing sticks. In Swedish, both the cross and the shed are called the "skäl".

DENTS: The spaces in the reed through which the warp ends are drawn.

DIENTES: A decorative border where wefts of two different colors alternate and create a striped effect. In Swedish, these are often called *tvist* or *staplar*, "stacks."

FLOATS: A term that indicates that threads, in the warp or weft or both, sit on top of the fabric in a certain section.

FLOOR RYA: A rug in the rya technique, woven with a sturdy warp and a weft that is beaten hard.

FLOSSA: A knotted technique with a dense, short pile.

HEDDLES: In Sweden, the most common heddles are Texsolv, white polyester loops with an eye in the middle that are suspended on the shafts. They keep each warp end in place and in the correct order.

INTERLACING POINTS: Where a warp end cross-es a weft pick.

LAMMS: Short and long lamms can be found in most Swedish looms, directly under the shafts. They connect the shafts and the treadles, deter-mine how the shafts will be lifted and sunk, and distribute the tension evenly across each shaft. The top lamms of a countermarch (highest up, directly over the shafts) are also a part of that loom's bal-ancing system.

LEASING STICKS: A pair of flat, thin sticks that hold the cross in place and in order, furthest back in the loom.

MEASURING THREAD: Used to measure out the length of a warp and facilitate warping.

NATURAL MATERIALS: In our work and this book we use almost exclusively "natural materi-als," i.e. organic fibers that come from plants and animals.

PICKS PER IN/CM: The number of weft picks per inch or cm in a weaving. This is controlled by the weaver's hand and how hard they beat with the beater. Written as PPCM or PPI.

PICK UP: The opposite of "throwing the shut-tle", insomuch that the weaver works in different sections of the warp simultaneously and uses their hands (or maybe a pick-up stick) instead of throwing a pick across the whole width of the warp with a shuttle.

PLAIN WEAVE: One of the three basic weave structures, the simplest and most compact, with the most interlacing points.

PRE-SLEYING: A preparatory step that roughly but evenly distributes the warp ends over the predetermined weaving breadth.

RADDLE: A tool that fills the same function as the reed in the pre-sleying step. However, a raddle is open, like a comb.

REED: Determines the sett. The reed sits in the beater and is the tool that actually beats the weft into the weaving. It is used twice in the preparation of a warp: first for pre-sleying and then for sleying.

RYA: A knotted technique with a long, lively pile.

RÖLAKAN: A picked weave structure in diagonal, checked, or freeform shapes.

SATIN: One of the three basic weave struc-tures, relatively loose. Has fewer interlacing points than the other basic structures and is a good choice when you want to emphasize a surface.

SELVEDGE ENDS: Warp ends furthest out on the edges of the weaving that stabilize that edge and/or create a binding edge where needed. For example, they may be floating selvedges or may consist of two pairs of warp ends threaded and sleyed together for big, thick rugs.

SETT: The number of ends per cm or inch. Written EPCM or EPI. Regulated by the reed.

SHAFTS: The wooden sticks behind the beater on which heddles are suspended. They determine the order of the warp ends. In combination with the treadles, the shafts divide the warp into different layers so that the weft can be shuttled in.

SHUTTLE WEAVING: One way to insert the weft between the warp ends and into the weaving is by throwing a shuttle with the weft yarn loaded onto it.

SLEYING: Drawing the warp ends through the reed. Determines the sett and divides the warp ends evenly over the predetermined weaving breadth.

SLITRYA: A variation of rya that is meant for a wall, a bed, or a sofa and is woven more softly and sparsely than a floor rya. As cozy as a blanket.

TABBY: In some weave structures, a shuttled weft is used to create a secure foundation for the more decorative pattern weft picks. Most often plain weave, which is called tabby when it is used in this manner. Some examples of structures in this book that use a tabby base are rya and halvdräll.

THREADING: The step that determines the order of the warp ends in the weaving and how each end will be lifted or sunk in each shed while weaving.

THREADING HOOK/SLEYING HOOK: A tool used to draw the warp ends through the heddle eyes and/or the reed dents.

THREADING DRAFT: The part of the draft that shows how each end should be threaded in the heddles.

TIE-UP: The part of the draft that shows which treadles should be tied to which shaft (via the lamms).

TREADLES: The treadles are tied to the short and long lamms on a countermarch, and depressing each treadle determines which shafts (and thereby which ends) will be raised and which will be lowered.

TREADLING DRAFT: The part of the draft that shows in which order the treadles should be treadled.

TWILL: One of the three basic weave structures, medium-compact. Has more interlacing points than plainweave but fewer than satin. Has a clear diagonal directionality.

TYING ON: The preparatory step in which the warp is tied onto the fabric beam stick, which stretches the warp and creates even tension throughout the warp.

WARP: The threads that are beamed on, threaded, and sleyed horizontally into the loom. The foundation of all weaving.

WARPING MILL: A device on which a weaver makes a warp, deciding its length and number of ends.

WARPING ORDER: Determines the order in which the warp ends should be wound so that they end up in the correct order in the loom. This is most easily expressed as a table. If the warp is of a single color and type of yarn, no warping order is needed.

WEAVE STRUCTURE: Describes how the warp and weft threads interact with each other. May also be called "weaving technique." The basic structures are plain weave, twill, and satin.

WEAVING DRAFT: An illustration that shows the threading order, the tie-up, the treadling order, as well as the drawdown, which shows how the threads interact in the woven cloth.

WEFT: The material that interlaces with the warp and consequently forms a woven structure.

WEFT-FACED REP: A variation of plain weave where the weft completely covers the warp.

Thanks to:
All the companies that sponsored yarn for the projects in this book: Växbo Lin, Ekelund: Linneväveriet i Hörred, Holma-Helsingland/Borgs, and Rauma Ullvarufabrik. We became even more enamored of your yarns after having woven with them for this book.

ARIANNA: Lisa Hartman, teacher and current colleague, and Tina Ignell, for making space for me in the weaving world. Thorborg and Hjördis (and Gunilla and Josabet), for taking good care of your looms so that they could be of use for my generation—I promise to do the same. Professor Koslin and Dr. Cowgill, for courage and advice. Studio Supersju makes it all possible. My parents, for being such excellent examples. Erik, for your confidence, your constant opinion-having, and the mathematics. To Axel and Bror: every pick, I throw for you, with love.

MIRIAM: Kim, Bettan, Lisa, Elisabeth, and all the other teachers at HV: you opened the world of weaving to me with masterly expertise and humble generosity. The Parkman/Lönneborg family: a continual creative chaos in the very best way. My colleagues in Studio Supersju, for the constant challenge and inspiration. Sarah and Christopher + Mackan and Carro, for lending us your fantastic homes and all the other friends who fill my life with dance, music, food, encouragement, support, and energy. Without you, no making! Matti—my dear.
Grandma Parkman (1932-2018). "My fingers are itching!" you said, frustrated, when I told you about my projects and you could no longer weave yourself. Thank you for the desire to create, and for the mountains; and thank you to all the generations of weavers who precede us and have passed on your knowledge and experience.